**public
address
system**

public address system
poster speeches by typographers

Editors: Paul Finn, Angharad Lewis,
Harriet Warden and Thom Winterburn

With contributions by John Grogan,
Ayesha Mohideen and Aidan Winterburn

images
Publishing

Contents

nd Specialists

ALES

I AM THE
LEADEN ARMY
THAT CONQUERS
THE WORLD.

I AM TYPE

Public Address

' ... prospectuses, catalogues and posters which shout aloud. Here is poetry this morning ... '

Guillaume Apollinaire, 1913

Preface

Public Address System got its name after a long session of word-throwing between the exhibition's organisers. When we finally hit upon Public Address System we knew we had the title that embodied the spirit of the collective endeavour. It works on a number of levels, summoning a vision of occasions where people gather to hear speech; it evokes the kind of technical language used to describe typography, its systems and rules; and the words also act as an alternative description for the medium of the poster itself. So there in the title we had the essence of what the Public Address System project is all about – speech, typography and posters.

Typography can mean very little to those uninitiated in its beauty and powers of communication, but the way typography is approached and handled reaches far into all areas of life. When you pick up a newspaper, look for a street sign or choose a package from a shelf your experience and decisions are being manipulated (for the good or bad) by typography. Typography makes us respond to it whether we know it or not and this is also true of speech and posters. They are a triumvirate of mighty communicators.

Derek Birdsall commented to us when we first discussed his participation in the Public Address System project, that he had been mulling over an idea for a poster since the 1960s and that Public Address System was his chance to realise it at last. The poster he eventually delivered is one of the most intriguing in the collection, challenging, as it does, every convention of how a poster is supposed to work.

There are posters in the Public Address System collection made from all manner of materials – from Perspex, to gold foil, to a collage, including torn book pages and a 7″ vinyl record. And of course paper of many varieties features widely. In fact every designer responded to our brief (to design an A2 poster that was a typographic interpretation of a speech) in a way that surpassed expectations and the outcome is a collection of highly innovative approaches to poster design.

It is our hope that this collection will serve to bring typography, its importance in visual culture and its power in everyday life to a wider audience. Public Address System has also been a chance for graphic designers and typographers to explore their art. What has emerged above all else is that far from being dry or retiring, typography arouses passion.

Public Address System was exhibited at the Henry Peacock Gallery (London) in January 2004 and at Grafik Europe (Berlin) in October 2004.

Speaking to Eyes
Angharad Lewis
Illustrated with examples of inspirational typographic posters.

Great typography is not just about letters printed on paper. The best can make words come to life, sing, spit or shout, set the nuance of words gently afloat or plough meaning across an empty expanse of paper. Posters are often where typography is at its most dynamic because it has to hail its reader from amongst the visual bluster and noise of the urban environment. It has not only to make people lift their eyes and take notice, but also to absorb some meaning in the time it takes for their bus to pull off.

There is a symbiotic relationship between typography and the poster. The one keeps the other developing. While advertising, direct marketing, the internet, and an increasingly product-led media is jeopardising the poster as a means of communication, these threats force the medium to work harder and challenge graphic designers to devise new ways of making it work. Innovative typography is part of the solution.

Similarly, typography benefits from the poster. Although typography must suit its medium (an ostentatious display face is no good for the body text of a book) developments in everyday typography are often prompted by the radical innovations allowed by working in the medium of posters.

Things have changed dramatically for typographers in the last twenty years. Digital typesetting and design have expanded the possibilities of what can be achieved by the designer working with type as much as the advent of photosetting in the early twentieth century, even as much as Gutenberg's invention of moveable type in the fifteenth century. There is still a place, however, for craft, analogue technology and handmade methods in typography, as the posters in Public Address System show. And some of

Experimental Jetset,
Stedelijk Museum CS poster 2004

Henrik Kubel, Graphic Poetry, from the
series Teaching Posters, Buckinghamshire
College 2003

the most exciting innovations are being made by those designers reinterpreting analogue methods as a way of moving the digital aesthetic forward.

When you first learn about the alphabet as a child it's about forging the mental leap between the sounds you make with your lungs, tongue and mouth and the shape of letters. Then you put those together to make language and communicate with others through speech, reading and writing. Speech is forever grafted to the shape of letters and words on the page and in the same way that a person's voice invests speech with emotion and meaning, so the way letters look invigorates the meaning of written and printed words.

For these reasons we asked the designers taking part in Public Address System to create typographic posters inspired by speeches. Typography embodies the unification of word and image, and to make a visual interpretation of a speech reinforces this relationship between the verbal and the visual further still. Posters were chosen as the most complete medium, for their position as the visual equivalent of a person making a speech – public, expressive and attention-grabbing.

The exhibition raises many interesting ideas about current typographic practice and the place of graphic design in contemporary visual culture. It aims to challenge received and uninformed notions about typography, to bring it to a new audience and to reveal what an expressive and thought-provoking contribution typography can make to the visual world.

For the designers and typographers who have participated in the exhibition, it has been an opportunity to create a piece of work that is free from the usual constraints that go hand-in-hand with commercial work. Many designers maintain a dialogue between the work they produce for paying clients and the more experimental, personal work they produce for themselves. Innovation and originality often relies on

Müller + Hesse, poster for Richard Paul Lohse: Konstruktive Gebrauchsgrafik at Museum für Gestaltung Zürich 1999

Ralph Schraivogel, Out of Print, poster for Museum für Gestaltung Zürich 2003

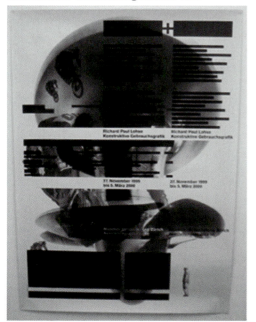

the nurturing of such work. Public Address System showcases the experimental, personal aspect of graphic design practice.

Throughout the preparation of the exhibition, four words from perhaps the most famous speech of modern times cropped up at every turn. They seemed to be the first reaction people had to the notion of famous speeches. It was tempting to ban them from the exhibition but when you stop and consider those four short words – I have a dream – they give an insight into the nature of speech making and highlight some of the reasons for staging this show.

The circumstances of that epoch-making speech paint a vivid picture. Martin Luther King led a peaceful march of 250 000 followers to the White House where he addressed the crowd. His words recalled the century-old promises of freedom made to black Americans, giving powerful resonance to the fact that as he spoke they lay unfulfilled. "So we have come here today to dramatise an appalling condition," he told the crowd. "We have also come to this hallowed spot to remind America of the fierce urgency of now." Then he made an optimistic plea for the future with those four legendary words. King's oratory was the epicentre of a historical moment that invoked the past and echoed into the future, sending out a powerful message to the world. Forty years later his words have become invested with a variety of meanings. 'I Have a Dream' has come to stand as an archetype of famous speeches and, although not many people could recite any more than those words, it has become a defining symbol of the civil rights movement in the collective consciousness.

It is interesting that all the exhibitors in this show have steered clear of King's speech. Perhaps there's a feeling that it's too widely known and too often recited to be run through the mill of interpretation yet again. Once a speech has been made, it exists in the public domain to be quoted (and misquoted), reeled off to reinforce an

Jonathan Barnbrook, posted around London the night before President George W Bush's visit 2003. Photographed by Fernando Cavalcanti.

Karl Gerstner, National Zeitung 1960. Photographed by Will Amlot at Fifty Posters, Spin Gallery 2004.

original point or corrupted for other means. It starts a journey of evolution and dilution in the mouths of others. Speeches dip in and out of public awareness, becoming quotes and slogans, aphorisms that embody the spirit of the original words or subvert and bend it to the will of a new speaker. Even when transcribed, the meaning of speeches fluctuates, and when there is no definitive record of what was said, word-of-mouth subjects the meaning to reinterpretation. Through the posters in Public Address System the words of the speeches chosen are brought into another stage of their evolution.

Posters have provided one of the most powerful ways of communicating messages for over a century. What makes the successful poster such a strong visual tool is its ability to express often complicated ideas in a succinct, engaging and public way. Alan Fletcher's poster in Public Address System (p. 61) is one of the most striking exhibits and shows poster design at its simplest and most dynamic, with words and image acting in perfect collusion. The composition and the blaring black on yellow palette make it the compelling visual equation of a shout.

Many of the posters evoke the audio and visual aspects of public demonstration. Red Design's (p. 99) displays two speeches, both given as troops embarked for the 2003 Iraq conflict – one delivered by a British commander and the other by a US Vice Admiral. The jaw-dropping contrast in the rhetoric of the two speakers is reinforced by the typographical treatment of the words. The relative diplomacy of the British speech is given an archaic, colonial feel and superimposed over this is the belligerent US speech, rendered in the style of fast-moving news sound-bite graphics.

As this poster highlights, today's era of political spin makes the speeches of leaders like Blair and Bush sound hollow and false, no more than highly polished PR exercises, while the kind of impassioned speech delivered by Martin Luther King in 1963 seems a paragon of deeply felt speechmaking.

**Robert Büchler, Typographie 1960.
Photographed by Will Amlot at Fifty
Posters, Spin Gallery 2004.**

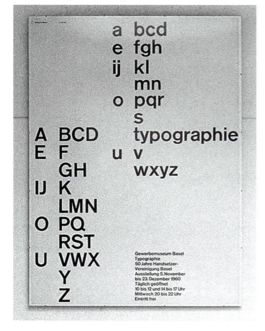

Designing posters specifically for display in an art gallery meant that Public Address System's designers were free to experiment with ideas perhaps impossible to implement in their commercial work. Sometimes this involved deliberately obscuring the text they reproduced as a way of exploring the properties of typography. For example Derek Birdsall's poster (p. 39) of Molly Bloom's soliloquy at the end of Joyce's Ulysses uses blocks of densely set type to reinforce the labyrinthine impenetrability of the prose style. Without intense scrutiny of the poster's surface it is impossible to read the type – a visual and physical parallel to the intellectual experience of reading and attempting to penetrate the meaning of Joyce's words.

The way type is set can also be symbolic, as is shown by the poster designed by Susanna Edwards and Martin McGrath (p. 49), a speech from a cockroach to NATO specially composed by poet Sexton Ming. The words are set in six-point type in the centre of the poster, requiring close-up interaction by the reader. As if giving visual form to the tiny voice of the cockroach, this treatment of the text also alludes to the futility of words, denoting the irony of this small voice speaking out so eloquently against the all-pervasive, anonymous power of a huge, unlistening authority.

The majority of the posters in Public Address System are purely typographical yet some contain an element of imagery. Paul Elliman's design (p. 53), a quote from Mary Shelley's Frankenstein, sits somewhere between the two. It uses the silhouetted shape of objects to denote letterforms. This treatment seems to find an echo in Frankenstein's creation of a monster from salvaged body parts and Elliman's own process of developing an alphabet from found objects. Erik Spiekermann's poster (p. 103) deals with the cultural identities attached to typefaces. It also points out parallels between the readability of visualised language and the linguistic obstacles in spoken language. It reproduces a speech by Mark Twain, The Awful German Language. The speech begins in English and lapses repeatedly into pidgin German

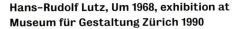
Hans-Rudolf Lutz, Um 1968, exhibition at
Museum für Gestaltung Zürich 1990

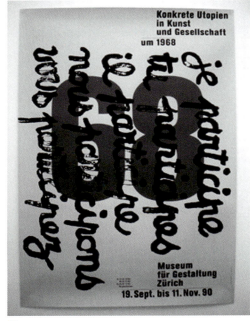

as Twain wrestles with language. The awkwardness of Twain's German phrases is reinforced by the use of hard-to-read Fraktur, making the viewer of the poster suffer the same linguistic discomfort that Twain inflicted on his own audience.

Each poster in the exhibition has its own point to make, both typographically and as a reflection of the personal choice of the designer in selecting their speech. They are typographical exercises, conceived to show how graphic design can amplify the meaning of written and spoken words and to point out the way that design is relevant, not only on a day-to-day level but also in addressing personal expression, poetry and politics. The exhibition contributes to the debate over how, and whether, we can still make clear-cut distinctions between graphic design and fine art. Fine art steps freely into the commercial realm to which graphic design is often confined, but the latter is rarely given the opportunity to engage with the fine art viewer. The place of good typography is on the pages of books and newspapers, on computer and movie screens and on the streets. I hope Public Address System goes some way towards showing that graphic design, both contemporary and historical, also befits the educational setting of a gallery.

Rather than art's poor cousin, it could be said that graphic design can have it both ways if we so choose: a maximum exposure where it functions in daily life, and a recognised place of value in the development of visual culture. Designer and writer Paul Rand said: "Typography is an art. Good typography is Art." Public Address System celebrates the beauty of typography and the resonance it has as a means of communication. It gives artists and designers, whose work is often only seen in a commercial context, the opportunity to create work to a non-commercial brief and exhibit in the democratic space of a gallery. By putting it in a contemporary art context, the viewer's cursory glance at graphic design is extended, hopefully eliciting an exploration of the processes of graphic design and typography and going some way to affirming its cultural value.

**Philippe Apeloig, The Poster,
Eastern Kentucky University 2000**

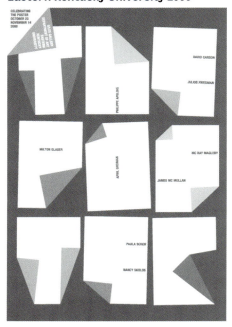

**G Klutsis, Let's fulfill the plan of Great Work
1930**

Politics is a Matter of Leading and Kerning

Aidan Winterburn

I reached something of a dilemma/impasse recently. I found myself bored by my constant reiterations about content over style. I railed like an old leftie against the spectacular productions of this consumerist, postmodern world, about the proliferation of surface over meaning, of the empty spectacle of visual production.

As I get older do I just get more naive? Style is everything – it's not what you do it's how you do it. Not empty style; style as parody, pastiche, sampling; as historicism or eclecticism. But style is political, style is subversive and, as Godard put it, "morality is a matter of tracking shots". So how did I get here to preaching the gospel of content? Am I falling into the game of separating the two, reinforcing those notions of 'designer' and 'content-provider'?

Like many people my age, my first contact with so-called typographic culture came through reading The Face in the 1980s. I read this latterly dubbed 'style bible' not to be dictated to about what I should be wearing, or listening to, or reading, but for a kind of refracting mirror to my own life. I'm not naive enough to really believe the magazine was a kind of passive document of a scene or a subculture, but through my rose-tinted specs (sorry, cool wraparound shades) there seemed to be more of a two way dialogue between the magazine and the audience. I didn't find myself in the pages nor did I really want to aspire to these kinds of roles (up in the provinces we clung dearly to the antiheroism of punk). I read the magazine because I wanted to read a Terry Hall interview, or an editorial piece by Julie Burchill, and, somewhere in the back of my mind, this was mediated by a vague sense of newness, of innovation, of something I had not seen before, by a new arrangement of words and images on the page.

I subsequently found out the debt that Neville Brody owed to the Constructivists and Italian Futurists and understood somewhere that this typography had a lineage that went back to the 'typo-photo' of Moholy-Nagy and El Lissitzky, that type had become a form of imagery for a kind of post-literate readership. These had already been touchstones for Peter Saville's work for Factory records and so my eye had become accustomed to these stylistic traits.[1] My dad made comments about the name Joy Division and attacked me for owning Everything's Gone Green, which traded on Neo-Fascist imagery. I was surprised by this tirade from a libertarian and progressive father and realised that style could have real political implications so that as I went to anti-Nazi rallies in the early 1980s, I could still own Belsen is a Gas by the Sex Pistols or ironically co-opt SS insignia on my Clash-type combat jacket. Suddenly I realised the power that the appropriation of Fascist iconography could have. What had remained if not invisible, then at least peripheral to my vision then started to gain centre ground. I started to realise the power of style to comment on, to subvert, to challenge and to resist.

I've often wondered about the way that design in the 1980s could be seen as being both critical of that "low and dishonest decade" (to borrow from Auden's memorable phrase), and complicit in its very nature. Is it possible to occupy both corners at the same time? For me, design made an implicit connection between the black years of the 30s and the 80s: through the appropriation of a neo Art Deco (Terry Farrell etc.) and the free-range ability to assimilate different styles, a new kind of Victorian eclecticism – the matt black functionalism of the Le Corbusier chaise longue, the co-option of both Fascist and Bolshevik imagery. The two decades are inextricably linked through

1 It seems strange to me that I am now talking about work that seems like ancient history and that has been inducted into the canon of the great and the good of design/typography.

boom and bust cycles, of political polarisation and the establishment of two Englands, a prosperous South and an ailing North. In this way, weren't designers making an explicit commentary on that decade in a way that eclipses those of say, Bonfire of the Vanities and Wall Street? So here we have style as political commentary, as both complicit in the selling of this consumerist, individualist free market economy and a subversive and critical chorus against it. It both reflected Thatcher's dynamic opening up of the market and at the same time dressed up the increasing social control that went to mask, obscure and delimit some of the social implications of those economic policies. I was fascinated by the way the typography of The Face could do both simultaneously, both to make people aware of the increasing split between the two Englands and at the same time cover over the cracks with consumer images, revelling in the loose and superficial interplay of surfaces and yet again, from the inside, critique these. Is this what Frederic Jameson meant when he talked of a kind of postmodern schizophrenia?[2]

When I was asked by the Henry Peacock Gallery to write a piece for Public Address System, I was interested to discover that much of the work eschewed both straight typographic treatment (are words not enough on their own? Is transparency a bad thing?) and any explicitly political polemic. This I found symptomatic of a particular design culture where style has been successfully extricated from either implicit or more explicit political and social concerns. How did this happen?

The modernism of the Bauhaus, and its derivatives at Ulm and later at the Illinois Institute of Technology, was based on strong utopian and idealistic notions of egalitarianism, of social democracy and social change. This was, of course, part of a tradition that stretches back to William Morris and which saw design as an outgrowth of moral, ethical, social and political concerns. Functionalism aimed to liberate man

2 I've often thought that the 80s could be defined by a kind of viral analogy. The HIV virus seemed particularly of its decade; whether it be Barbara Kruger taking over the host body – advertising, films like Blue Velvet and The Fly, or the deconstructive urge of Eisenman and Derrida and Tschumi. These seem to recognise the need to engage with commerce and somehow to infect the host body, allowing the virus to incubate/subvert at a later stage. As Dick Hebdige writes in his article 'The Bottom Line on Planet One' from 'Hiding in the Light', The Face was "hyperconformist, more commercial than commercial, more banal than banal".

through the provision of basic needs, the impartiality of objectively, rationally designed communications, the production of an adaptable and flexible environment that responded to new forms of living. The designer became a kind of engineer of design solutions that would encourage new ways of living, in the sense of becoming a new kind of engineer of the soul (with all the crypto-Fascistic overtones that this brings with it). Design became an analysis of needs – a rationalist equation where the most reduced and the simplest always functioned best. And its critics of course scorned its clinical products, its anonymity, and its functionalism. Style was international at a time when nationalism threatened to tear Europe apart. Functionalism was proclaimed at the same time as what Raymond Williams saw as a third stage of commodity production which emphasised the "non-rational symbolic grounding of consumption", where advertising became an integral definer of consumer demand and an important means of controlling the market. Of course much of this International Style, although predicated on rationalism and function, was poetic and aesthetic and maybe we should regard Le Corbusier and Tschichold's similar proselytising in 'Vers Une Architecture' and 'Die Neue Typographie' as being largely disingenuous, caught up in a seductive and modish fetishisation of the machine aesthetic. Although this was never really properly articulated, it became a kind of self-perpetuating argument, a way of simply using zeitgeist as an overarching defence.

Still there is something heroic and noble here. Bayer's overhaul of Germanic black-letter forms in favour of a thoroughly minimalist and rationalist lower case Bauhaus typeface that suggested a 'root and branch' reform of typographic production and design, his disavowal of Nazi 'blut und boden' folkish vernacular, is a high watermark of typography as politically charged discourse. Of course Bayer was instrumental in bringing the International Style to the US where it was, at times, enthusiastically received as an expression of a new world super-power in the Cold War, as a kind of propaganda tool to express both the good taste and seriousness of postwar multinational corporatism and the innovation, sophistication, modernity and freedom of American society.[3]

Walter Gropius went to Harvard, and Mies van der Rohe built the Seagram building, which saw the wholesale co-option of continental modernism by the US. This was the beginning of the way that design was slowly stripped of its original social, left-wing tendencies, which were incorporated into American capitalism and co-opted by Madison Avenue and Hollywood.

In England of course, modernism was adopted by a new Welfare State for housing and industrial design. It seemed to speak of a new egalitarian society so that all manner of governmental initiatives to encourage 'good design' through the Design Council were established. We're still living through this fall-out. On the one hand modernism is tarred with the tower block and on the other with the corporate headquarters, the road sign and the company annual report. And so we question whether this was really where modernism was always heading. Was it inevitable that capitalism would co-opt these dangerous tendencies and blunt their impact? In Walter Benjamin's words, it would always be able to "assimilate revolutionary themes, indeed propagate them without calling its own existence and the class that owns it seriously into question". Is there a different modernism, a forgotten modernism?

I've wondered about how literary modernism stands at odds with elements of visual modernism and the position of Dada/Futurism/Vorticism within this, operating as a kind of guerrilla warfare in the fields of modernism. And so we have Pop Art as a neo Dada and Young Brit Art as a neo neo neo Dada. Was Pop Art the disjuncture here, where design resigned itself to giving up the utopian dream and faced reality by plumping for Main Street, Sunset Strip and the shopping mall? Or were these the ghosts in the work

3 Interestingly Modernist typographers had few problems in transferring their skills to the selling of capitalist products; they simply emphasised the need for rational and clear communication of products and services as a public good.

of the first modernists Baudelaire and Manet? Is Warhol's blankness that of the woman depicted in Bar at the Folies Bergeres? Whatever.

Are we at the end of politics? Is this the end of ideology? If this is the end of the big meta-narratives, the end of the big stories that have organised our lives, we cannot believe in politics, either personal or party. You might counter this and say there has been an upsurge in popular political engagement with the campaigns against the war in Iraq and the anti-corporate movement. Are these truly political? Or more ethical in character? What perhaps unites these campaigns is the broad spectrum of support they engender. These are private acts of conscience that have no greater political perspective. This is perhaps reflected in the territorial skirmishes witnessed recently between graphic designers over the First Things First manifesto of 2000. This manifesto had been appropriated from Ken Garland's original in 1965. There was a kind of protestant revulsion from, in Hoggart's terms, "the Candy Floss World" of advertising and consumerism. Its co-option in the late 1990s suggests that there is some revisiting of the 1960s (for swinging London read Britpop/art etc.) that is perhaps evidenced by Adbusters' neo Situationist detournements. Interestingly, the revisited manifesto sparked off something of a dispute between the editor of Adbusters, Kalle Lasn, and Chomsky's co-author of 'Manufacturing Consent', Edward Herman, when Herman accused Adbusters of empty sloganeering and lacking a true political perspective. This ended in Lasn deriding Herman for being "a traditional Leftie" who seemed happy to describe as action such efforts as "thinking very hard" and writing proposals that others are expected to carry forward. These minor altercations suggest a kind of naivety on both parts. There is the old social conscience school, represented by those such as Katherine McCoy's 'issue-oriented work' at Cranbrook Academy, the idea of doing "one for the bank balance and one for the soul".

What is politically correct work? Statements like Jonathan Barnbrook's billboard for Adbusters at the AIGA's conference in Las Vegas announcing "Designers; stay away from corporations that want you to lie for them", and "designers are actually the foot soldiers of capitalism", seem to confirm a kind of political naivety. This perhaps attributes too much power to the designer as explicit political agent. As an antidote to this, Milton Glaser regards the designer as acting purely as an intermediary, as he puts it, "the rules are being written but not by designers … they don't make the determinations they don't decide what is to be sold … their role has become a mediation between clients and audience where they act more like telephone lines than like initiators".

The designer is powerless in the face of corporate power. As Emily King remarks in her analysis of Brody's Fuse project, envisaging the end of politics, "today's celebrity designer seems to assume himself helpless". So how would I design an anti-war poster in this light? Would I fall in with the old leftist oppositional tactics, make worthy statements, or culture jam, use a form of cultural jiu-jitsu, march quietly through the institutions?

So to talk about typography being political is a nonsense. We are cut adrift to browse and graze across, to swallow and regurgitate different styles that repeat on us as pure aesthetic, without moral, political foundation. We are granted a kind of phantasmagoria of styles and devices and techniques. If I am not constrained by the demands of audience, of technology, of budget, of my own skills, everything is flattened into a meaningless landscape where everything is permitted but nothing is meaningful. If the Dadaists were forced to use old type slugs from various fonts to produce their pamphlets and posters, if the Constructivists' montage cinema came out of both the theoretical position of dialectical Marxism with the constraints of short ends of film stock that had to be pasted together, what does the promise of absolute freedom and

plenitude that the computer promises mean for the designer/typographer?[4] We can browse through different eras, styles, surfaces, but they're not used straight or ironically, but somewhere in between, blankly. As Kaplan says we are offered "timeless perpetual presents ransacking history". They're not used as homage or as pastiche, but simply because you can. The relationship between design and the political, the social is cut loose, even the postmodern negation of the negation. As Barbara Kruger says, "everything is consumed by style which is socially constructed and grants power and takes it away". Styles become clothes to try on and then discard – the recent return to an aesthetic modernism becoming the last laugh of postmodernism[5] all of it signifying nothing other than the good taste of the reader, the user, the consumer. Mai '68 stencilled letter forms are used to sell Nike trainers and the perpetuation of styles turns into Cold War-like escalation. The big guns are brought out, shock, sex, horror, the bizarre and each successive style and aesthetic becomes a hollow spectacle that must keep raising the ante.[6] Both aim at a kind of hermetic seamlessness that disavows criticism and nit-picking. This neo-mania reflects consumer society's endless need for novelty and its unquenchable passion for making undeliverable promises about lifestyle, belonging, status, sex and money – promises it must endlessly defer. Design becomes a lifestyle choice, it confirms the illusory freedom society promises us. I can live in a loft apartment with my Eames Ottoman and my Eileen Grey table that I keep my style magazines on. The working class can have their Argos catalogues and their dado rails, their curlicues and Easyjet…

We have to accept that capitalism has managed to provide us with a neutered modernism. Here we are: a selection of typographers who seem unhappy with their lowly trade and aspire to the conditions of fine art. I am disappointed by this – is it too much for designers to have the confidence to simply lay out the words in a way that foregrounds

4 As Jon Wozencroft remarks in Fuse, "the more sophisticated all of these communication technologies become, the harder it is to actually communicate. Technology promises freedom, it only delivers frustration".

5 With the double–coding of Jencks, where one part modern is mixed with something more populist/historical becomes one part modern with another part modern.

6 There is a delicious irony that advertising and modern art have both been "intent on controlling the ground" to produce a visual hegemony through the same strategies and tactics if not the same techniques.

the meaning? Can't the type remain transparent and through this quietism work on the periphery of my vision? Why must it shout over the words? Was this a holiday from the rigours of 'work'? Did this represent an escape into spurious ideas of self-expression and freedom, or, as Emily King says about Neville Brody's Fuse project it simply reflects "displays of professional virtuosity… the designer defining a territory that he can occupy unchallenged."

The Illumination of the Familiar
Ayesha Mohideen

In the sea of words that surrounds us, some float to the top. They are the same and yet different. They distinguish themselves from the idle chatter of friends or the background babble of the radio, not because they are intrinsically different, but because their potency in combination arrests our attention, even burns them on to our brains. It is not particularly surprising, but still somehow remarkable that, though I cannot remember the first thing I said yesterday, I can recognise the words of a prime minister, who died a decade before I was born, spoken to rouse a nation during a war I never knew. It is not simply their repetition that awards great speeches a legacy that outlives their makers, nor the significance of the events which they describe, but some inherent quality that makes them worthy of such repetition in the first place.

Constantly, we seek words to anchor time. Though powerless to prevent its passage, we nonetheless look to restrain its progress somehow: keeping a diary, sending a card, looking for the right words to leave a mark on a moment, big or small. In turn, we seek to capture words themselves, to preserve memories or pass on culture, learning and thought: storing them in books, crystallising them in recordings, committing them to memory. To that end, to choose images as a means to commemorate the extraordinary force of words is not as oxymoronic as it might appear. The images extend and explore the strength of the words, as you will see. For instance in Alan Kitching's intensely vivid evocation of Winston Churchill's first speech as prime minister to the Commons in 1940 (p. 77).

You will find almost every manifestation of speech in this collection of posters: from song to script, from poem to proverb, from lecture to literature. The result is the

illumination of the familiar, casting fresh light on our language. These unions of words and images invite comparison with the unions of linguistic styles so often deployed by some of the most illustrious orators of our time. It calls to mind Bill Clinton, the politician as preacher, audaciously addressing an audience of no fewer than five thousand ministers in 1993 from the pulpit of the Baptist church in Memphis where Martin Luther King delivered his last sermon. Famously departing from his script to borrow the language of his audience and his upbringing, he extemporised an ardent call to action to honour King's legacy. It calls to mind Churchill, whose speeches were typed psalm-style, with the text indented, creating steps down the length of the page.

The period from Churchill to Clinton is one that has witnessed an unprecedented change in the nature of public address. Churchill was a noted exponent of the mass medium of broadcasting, seizing on its capacity to take his message to millions simultaneously. From then on, a speech could be heard as it was intended, not read later in a newspaper. The speaker's voice became as important as his or her words, if not more so, a factor which has helped to shape the modern politician. With the advent of television, millions could experience the oratory almost first-hand. At that point, the importance of those actually experiencing the oratory first-hand diminished. For speakers, the audience they could not see superseded the audience they could. Speeches were written for the public at large, rather than those who actually chose to go and hear them. It is the news bulletin that now gives the political party conference its point, not the political party.

The mass media have elevated oratory to some degree, magnifying its impact as one person's words can ricochet around the world. Can any single person have been heard by so many others at once as when, at the funeral of his sister in 1997, Earl Spencer gave voice to his grief and anger before the world, smashing convention as he did so? His

words reverberated through Westminster Abbey and beyond, so affecting the audience he could not see in the streets and open spaces outside that they began to applaud. As the sound of their applause reached the Abbey, the congregation joined in, that moment epitomising the widest point of the rift between the monarch and her subjects that opened up when the Princess of Wales died.

Their appearance in our living rooms means we feel we have come in some way, to know the public figures of our time as never before. Yet there is a question as to whether this familiarity has rendered those in public life larger or smaller. Modern broadcasting has an insatiable appetite for material but it is less the set-piece speech that flourishes in this environment and more the hard-edged interview, the ad hoc comment to a waiting press pack, the cut and thrust of a press conference. Two hundred years ago, a major figure might only give a speech on a handful of occasions a year, delivering a meticulously crafted oration to a waiting audience; today's public figure must offer opinions on demand or risk no audience at all. A different skill is called for involving improvisation, variations on a theme and speed of thought. For such a figure, the combination of modern broadcasting, modern mores and opinions on demand can result in the spontaneous brilliance of a one-liner or the oft-repeated humiliation of a 'gaffe'. Simon Waterfall (p. 107) recalls precisely this in his poster, proving that though more than a decade has passed since Gerald Ratner gave his now infamous speech to the Institute of Directors, it is far from forgotten.

However, no humiliation was perhaps as immense as that endured by Clinton, when the most powerful man in the world was, by his conduct, made small before the world. His brief address to the nation in 1998, admitting an inappropriate relationship with a White House intern, saw him both acknowledging and railing against his indignity, trapped by his opponents in the unprecedented glare of the public eye.

Of course, what we say, inadvertently or otherwise, is sometimes less interesting than what we do not. We dissect public pronouncements to find out what they 'really' mean; we conduct imaginary arguments in our heads; we bite back words that betray our emotions. However, it is the words we hope never to hear that Michael Morrisoe explores in his searingly affecting poster of the speech Richard Nixon had written for him in the event of disaster befalling the moon landings (p. 87). Finding the words for a suffering people that articulate their angst, yet offer them hope, is perhaps the heaviest responsibility of a public figure. It is not surprising that in these circumstances, they often turn to a professional.

Nixon had chosen William Safire to be his speechwriter, who was to become one of America's most eminent newspaper columnists. He occupied that most curious of roles which requires the regular conjuring trick of putting words into someone else's mouth that aspire to better than their own, while appearing to be entirely their own. Having fulfilled this role myself (to far less eminent effect, it must be said), I can vouch for the fact that while it may be curious, it is certainly fascinating. To pull off the trick offers only a secret satisfaction because the illusion of ownership must usually be maintained. Yet there is indeed satisfaction to be derived from having successfully found someone else's voice and given it new words. It is a fine line between finding that voice and mimicking it: the words must have an authenticity that does not belie their origin and must play to the speaker's values as well as his or her rhetorical strengths. Once those words are delivered or quoted in newspapers, they cease to be one's own and become the property of the speaker, given that the power of oratory is in the delivery, perhaps even more than in the words themselves. The fact that Ronald Reagan's words were often put into his mouth by his talented speechwriter, Peggy Noonan, did not, in effect, detract from his ability to touch the American people with them.

However, it is hard not to let the origin of a speaker's words form part of one's assessment of that speaker. Indeed, sometimes the very fact that they have not been written at all lends them more influence. Clinton and King both exercised the gift of ex tempore oratory to commanding effect, as did Neil Kinnock in one of his most memorable speeches about his socialism "Why am I the first Kinnock in a thousand generations to be able to get to university?" I make no apology for mentioning Kinnock in the same sentence as these more widely celebrated practitioners of the art of speech making. It is unfortunate that Kinnock's contribution to public discourse is so often caricatured as pure "windbaggery", given that he is probably the most skilful British public speaker of his time. His lack of electoral success, especially when contrasted with Margaret Thatcher's own oratory, perhaps serves only to illustrate that although forceful public speaking can move the minds of millions, there is no guarantee that it will.

The power of public pronouncement is extensively explored in this exhibition, much of which looks at the political sphere. The most contemporary example sees the overlaying of the speeches to US and UK troops on the eve of the war with Iraq, to devastating effect. Although both forms of propaganda in their own ways, the blunter instrument of the American Vice Admiral when contrasted with Lieutenant Colonel Tim Collins' address, which has become one of the most memorable speeches of the new decade, itself demonstrates the importance of the spoken word in moving and motivating millions.

However, for all the focus on the impact of oratory, it is worth remembering that sea of words with which we started. Morag Myerscough's elevation of the ordinary in her 'Replacing speech: two years worth of text messages' is a reminder of the way in which words move us on a daily basis, as anyone who has ever sat waiting for the phone to ring – or bleep – knows (p. 89).

It is impossible for us to conceive of a world without words, just as impossible as it is for us to conceive of a world without images. Fusing them together, as the contributors to this exhibition have done, is to create at times an extraordinarily powerful expression of what it is to be human, from the mundane to the momentous.

A Good Speech: Tips from a Backbench MP

John Grogan MP

Power Point is the scourge of good speeches. Why not email everyone a handout and save on the human contact? How often have you been sat half way back in a dimly lit hall straining your eyes to try and make out the blurred lettering on the screen? Visual aids have become the master of too many speechmakers rather than the servant they were always meant to be. Tip number one is to use such aids sparingly, which will in any event maximise their impact.

Secondly, it is just common courtesy to think about your audience and address yourself specifically to them. After all those who on a date use the same chat up lines whoever they are out with and show little real interest in the other person generally, end up looking rather stale and shallow. The same is true of the speaker who, however eminent, gets lazy and gives much the same speech whatever his or her audience. One job of a guest speaker is to help define the occasion and give people a reason for being there. This is as true of opening a village fete as it is of the Budget speech. I once heard a thirty-minute oration from a household name addressing an audience entirely made up of publicans. The star guest failed to mention beer once and was about as popular as a best man at a wedding who insists on telling one boorish and laddish joke after another much to the discomfiture of the elderly relatives.

Thirdly, if you can pull it off, a bit of humour goes a long way. Always remember that a joke or story will go down all the better if it is appropriate to the audience and

to the general theme of the speech. A good speech should be more than a string of gags. The key is to weave humour into the general theme of the speech so that it reinforces the central message.

A beginning, a middle and an end is always a good idea. The opening paragraph of a speech, if not the opening line, should clearly specify the theme. I well recall former Labour Prime Minister Jim Callaghan speaking at an election rally in Leeds Town Hall, saying he felt at home and pointing to a Latin inscription on the wall which read 'Labor Omnia Vincit' (Labour conquers all). In one line he had established a theme and a sense of place and his audience were listening. On the other hand a conclusion should encapsulate exactly what it is you want the audience to take away with them.

Good speechmaking is an act of theatre. If you get the chance it is always worth taking a few minutes to acclimatise at the venue before the action starts. Just basics like checking that the microphone is the correct height and there is somewhere to put your notes can help calm your nerves. In the House of Commons I always like to speak from the back row. This is not primarily so that I can make a speedy exit if things go wrong but just because I find it easier from there to project my voice and attempt to command the attention of the House.

If preparation time is limited for a speech and your knowledge of the subject somewhat sparse, there is only one remedy – turn up early and talk to people and find out what's what! It is much more interesting to your audience if you are opening, say, an extension to a sports club if you can say something about that club. Point to a plaque on the wall which commemorates the work of the founder of the club, refer authoritatively to the exact year that the team won the league, wish the juniors well in their first match of the season against named opposition. All this is far more personal and relevant than waffling generalities.

So many speeches now come packaged as part of a meal. I hate after-dinner speaking if it means sitting for hours talking politely to your neighbour and picking away at food you have no appetite for. If you share my nervous disposition why not ask to speak after the first course so that you can relax and enjoy the rest of the event. I got this tip by the way from none other than the Speaker of the House of Commons, Michael Martin.

If you make a mistake all you can do is to try and maintain your composure and avoid becoming flustered. I was recently making an impassioned address to the nation's Parliament urging the case for more Bank Holidays. Making a comparison with the number of holidays enjoyed by some of our European Union neighbours I got rather too excited and apparently made a rallying call not for 'Bank Holidays' but for 'Bonk Holidays'! Living to fight another day is sometimes all you can hope for.

Speaking of passion, I think that, along with the aforementioned humour, raw brutal honesty is one of the three most powerful ingredients of any speech. So long as it is not obviously false an audience will generally respond to someone who speaks, whether in a soft or a powerful voice, with strong conviction or belief. Perhaps even more effective is the simple, direct display of honesty. Sometimes the most memorable speech at a wedding is not the long address given by a practised speaker but the unscripted remarks of a father or a friend who may never have given a speech before but whose words resonate with emotion and affection.

I AM THE
LEADEN ARMY
THAT CONQUERS
THE WORLD:

I AM TYPE

Public Addr

HENRY PEACOCK
GALLERY
WED-SAT   12-6

You can dictate
just about anywhere
you can type.

ss System

Derek Birdsall
**Molly Bloom's soliloquy
James Joyce: Ulysses 1921**

Molly Bloom's soliloquy from the end of Ulysses by James Joyce   typography Derek Birdsall 2002

The Dignity of Human Labour
Phil Oakey, The Human
League 1979

The text for the poster is from a flexi-disc
that came with an early Human League 12"
called The Dignity of Labour (Parts 1–4).
The actual music is very abstract and
gloomy, but the flexi-disc is hilarious. It
features a long argument between the
band and their manager about what they
should include on the flexi-disc! It ends
with Phil Oakey, the asymmetric lead
singer, reading out his "heavy statement".

I chose this text for its deadpan humour.
It reads like earnest sixth form poetry,
but I think the actual philosophy behind it
makes sense!

The design of the poster is very simple and
uses antique Letraset in homage to early
Human League sleeves.

WHAT WE'VE GOT IN THIS IS NOT SIMPLE
LIKE EVERYTHING ELSE AND IT'S NOT EVEN COMPLEX,
IT'S MULTIPLEX.

THE PICTURE OF YURI GAGARIN ISN'T ABOUT RUSSIAN SOCIETY,
AND IT'S NOT JUST ABOUT THE RUSSIAN SPACE EFFORT.
IT IS ABOUT THE INDIVIDUAL AS OPPOSED TO THE GROUP,
AND IT'S ABOUT HUMAN HUMAN FRAILTY.
NO MATTER HOW BIG YOU ARE,
YOU'RE GOING TO BE DEAD PRETTY SOON.

PHILIP OAKEY
APRIL 1979

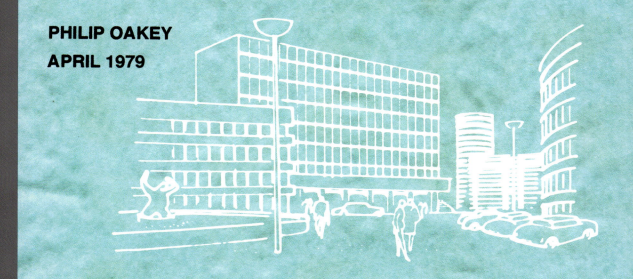

Margaret Calvert
Major's speech to the comrades of Animal Farm
George Orwell: Animal Farm 1946

Major's speech to the comrades of Animal Farm, delivered live on BBC World Service, at 1.05am London time, confirmed my choice, having spent a restless couple of hours trying to remember a political speech which was both timeless and would suit my approach.

This particular transmission, produced by Nick Runkin in 'Masterpiece', was initially programmed to be broadcast in May 1982, but was blocked by The National Theatre because of copyright reasons. The first public broadcast was adapted by George Orwell for a schools' broadcast of Animal Farm in 1946, soon after he left the BBC.

I like to think that the sum of its parts, including the bulldog clips, and the appro-priation of a page lifted directly from a special edition of Animal Farm (published by Penguin in 2003 to celebrate Orwell's Centenary) reflect Orwell's parody of

Soviet Russia and, with his reference to "the gramophone mind", his political stance. The visual concept was inspired by El Lissitzky's Beat the Whites with the Red Wedge executed in 1919.

'I have little more to say. I merely repeat, remember always your duty of enmity towards Man and all his ways. Whatever goes upon two legs is an enemy. Whatever goes upon four legs, or has wings, is a friend. And remember also that in fighting against Man, we must not come to resemble him. Even when you have conquered him, do not adopt his vices. No animal must ever live in a house, or sleep in a bed, or wear clothes, or drink alcohol, or smoke tobacco, or touch money, or engage in trade. All the habits of Man are evil. And above all, no animal must ever tyrannize over his own kind. Weak or strong, clever or simple, we are all brothers. No animal must ever kill any other animal.
BUT SOME ARE MORE
'And now, comrades, I will tell you about
night. I cannot describe that dream to you. It was a dream of the earth as it will be when Man has vanished. But it reminded me of something that I had long forgotten. Many years ago, when I was a little pig, my mother and the other sows used to sing an old song of which they knew only the tune and the first three words. I had known that tune in my infancy, but it had long since passed out of my mind. Last night, however, it came back to me in my dream. And what is more, the words of the song also came back – words, I am certain, which were sung by the animals of long ago and have been lost to memory for generations. I will sing you that song now, comrades. I am old and my voice is hoarse, but when I have taught you the tune you can sing it better for yourselves. It is called "Beasts of England".'
Old Major cleared his throat and began to sing. As he had said, his voice was hoarse, but he sang well enough, and it was a stirring tune, something between 'Clementine' and 'La Cucuracha'. The words ran:

Cathal Connaughton

Inspired by a letter by Charles Dickens 1853

1853
Charles Dickens wrote "All work and no play may make Peter a dull boy as well as Jack". Although the wording is different, this is the first recorded use of the phrase. It was probably a proverb in common use in London at the time.

1854
The shortened "All work and no play makes Jack a dull boy" appears in Dickens' Hard Times.

1980
Stanley Kubrick's horror classic The Shining features the most famous appearance of the proverb. It is repeated over and over in different typographic configurations as Jack Nicholson's character descends into madness.

2003
In the six months leading up to the 24th November, I used 382 Post-it® Notes. These were collected and used to create the poster.

The photography for the poster is by Ture Anderson (A/P/O/G/S)

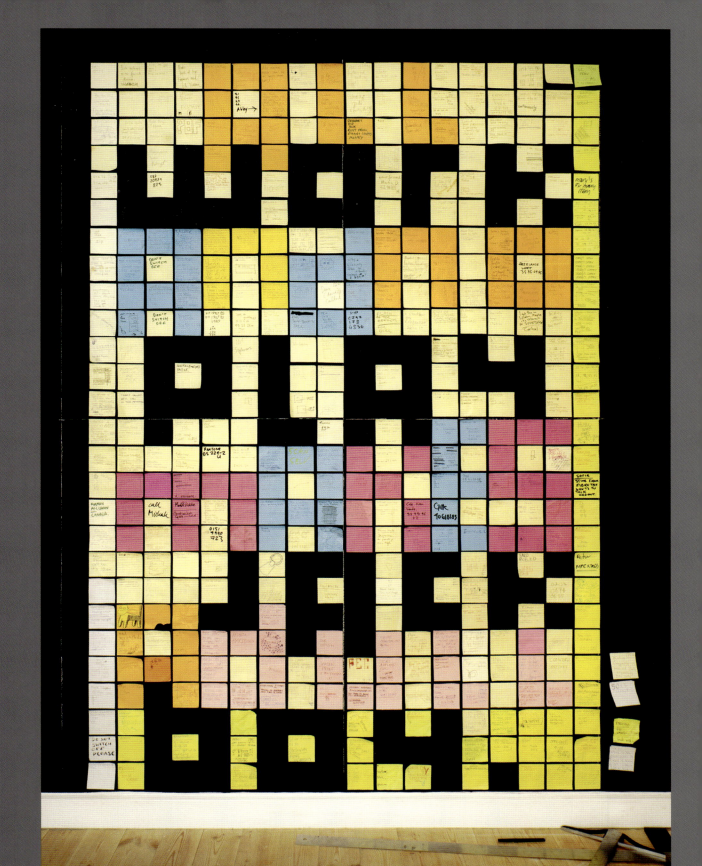

We Are All Prostitutes
Mark Stewart, The Pop Group
1979

The God-like genius of Mark Stewart and
The Pop Group.

100/100   mitDR

Susanna Edwards and Martin McGrath
Speech From a Cockroach to NATO, Sexton Ming 2003

Through brainstorming for this brief we came to the conclusion that we didn't want to illustrate the obvious. We approached the poet/artist/musician Sexton Ming to create a speech for us to work with. The speech therefore had an element of the unknown. Much to our delight Sexton created a speech from a Cockroach to NATO. The content of the speech led to our chosen medium of letterpress. It was agreed that the use of craft was more appropriate than a digitally designed piece of work. A very simple use of 6 point Baskerville set in the middle of an A2 poster is our finished design. The speech is unreadable from a distance. The tiny yet determined voice of Ricky the Cockroach has to be discovered by the viewer.

RICKY THE COCKY COCKROACH SPEECH TO N.A.T.O.

Hi there.

Us cockroaches and other insects have asked me to

encourage you at N.A.T.O. to have an all out nuclear war.

You don't even need a war if you don't want one.

Just nuke the planet.

You see, us cockroaches can take big cold and mighty heat.

You humans will die but we will survive.

We want the planet for ourselves as a playground

and somewhere to develop our species.

You have had a good run for your money...

Now it's our turn.

Yours with a warm hand shake

Ricky the cocky cockroach.

Jonathan Ellery
Speech at the Waldorf Astoria Hotel, New York Muhammad Ali September 1974

I don't have many heroes, but Mohammad Ali is one of them. His delivery of words in a pressurised sporting arena has always stood out for me, so the choice of speech was easy.

The text itself was sourced from the documentary When We Were Kings, directed by Leon Gast in 1996.

A lot of my recent graphic work explores the tactile qualities of traditional printing processes, taking something that's forgotten or perceived as being old-fashioned and putting it into a contemporary art context. The poster was gold foil-blocked onto four different materials.

Muhammad Ali

Waldorf Astoria Hotel
New York City
September 1974

Designed by Jonathan Ellery
Limited edition run of thirty

Henry Peacock Gallery
London 2004

I DONE WRASSLED WITH AN ALLIGATOR, I DONE TUSSLED WITH A WHALE, I DONE HANDCUFFED LIGHTNING. THROWN THUNDER IN JAIL, THAT'S BAD. ONLY LAST WEEK I MURDERED A ROCK. INJURED A STONE, HOSPITALIZED A BRICK. I'M SO MEAN I MAKE MEDICINE SICK.

Paul Elliman

**I Will Work At Your Destruction
Mary Shelley: Frankenstein
1818**

I Will Work At Your Destruction is a small
part of the creature's speech from Mary
Shelley's Frankenstein. I set it in my Bits
type, which I hope corresponds a little with
Shelley's story about a man built out of
waste parts, torn between a child-like
wonder at the world, and blind murderous
anger – part sensitive being, part machine,
completely out of control.

I WILL WORK AT YOUR DESTRUCTION

No Poetry to Recite
Stefan Themerson: Bayamus and the Theatre of Semantic Poetry 1949

A few months ago we were at a screening of an old Dutch television documentary from the 1970s, entitled 'Stefan Themerson en de Taal' (Stefan Themersonon Language). In one of the scenes, the Polish-born writer, film maker, publisher and poet Stefan Themerson (1910–1988) is shown reciting a paragraph from his novel Bayamus and the Theatre of Semantic Poetry (1949):

"My lord archbishop; your excellencies, your graces; my lords, ladies and gentle-men, men and women, children; embryos, if any; spermatozoa reclining at the edge of your chairs; all living cells; bacteria; viruses; molecules of air, and dust, and water… I feel much honoured in being asked to address you all, and to recite poetry – but I have no poetry to recite."

A beautiful, anti-climactic speech.

For our poster, we treated this speech in a somewhat analytical manner; by listing the addressees in a vertical way, we tried to emphasise the strong hierarchical logic behind the quote.

my lord archbishop
your excellencies
your graces
my lords
ladies **and**
gentlemen
men **and**
women
children
embryos **if any**
spermatozoa **reclining**
at the
edge
of your
chairs

all living cells
bacteria
viruses
molecules **of air and**
dust and
water,

i feel much honoured in being asked to address you all
and to recite poetry – but i have no poetry to recite.

stefan themerson 49
eksperimental jetset 03

Paul Finn
**Together We Are Robots
The United States of the
United Kingdom (USUK) 2003**

I was going to work one morning and had a horrible realisation that I was a robot. Hundreds of us in our conditioned realities carry out our programmed lives. I got to work, turned on my computer, put on my headphones and carried out my tasks until my Outlook calendar told me to go to another brain-melting meeting where other robots told me what I will be doing for the next four months...

At the time I was reading George Orwell's 1984, it was amazing how right he was back then in 1949. It prompted this poster. The truths which the book spoke completely amazed me: how words and their meaning can be controlled. So this was an attempt to suggest some future inauguration speech by a president robot figure in an attempt to prompt unity and boost morale for the new world order. He speaks from some masonic temple balcony to thousands of scared robots "Together We Are Robots" and is greeted with cheers.

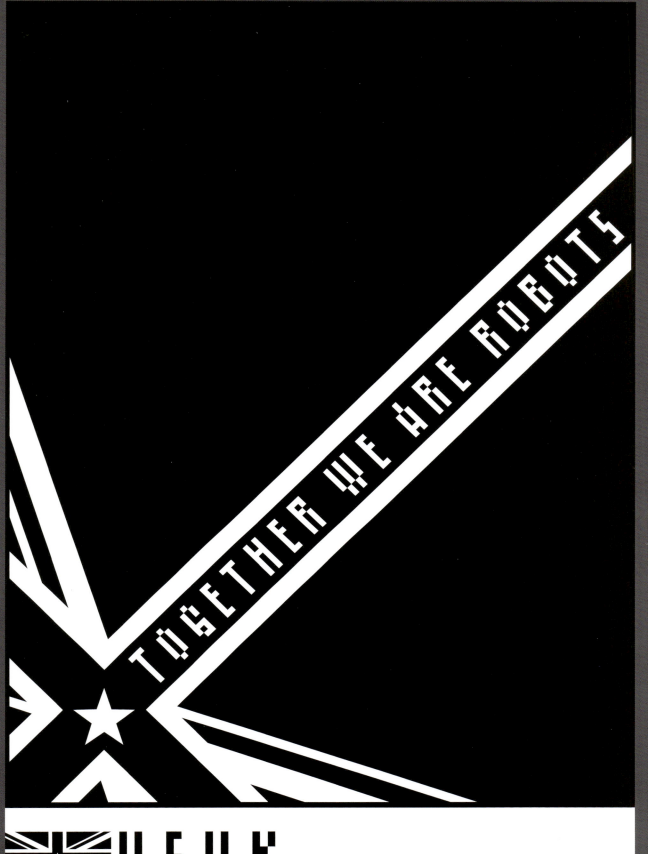

Fl@33

Address to the European Parliament
His Holiness the Dalai Lama
24 October 2001

Besides his report of the non-violent struggle of Tibet for independence from China, Dalai Lama focused on his annual claim for world peace. He described the global interdependence and suggested the improvement of mankind's "universal responsibility" beyond nations and religions. The poster presents the text in its entirety. While maintaining the Tibetan situation within the speech, more common aspects of world peace are highlighted with a marker-like fluorescent orange.

The poster is designed with three levels of accessibility. The form text is shaping a Quentin Tarantino-like situation of three armed men pointing their weapons at each other, forming a circle of violence. The silhouettes are showing warriors of different ages implementing the ongoing failure of mankind to achieve world peace. The highlights represent the second level to engage the curious viewer to step closer and read. Once the highlighted sentences and fragments summarise the speech, the audience might be intrigued enough to explore the complete text.

One aspect of the minimal poster concept reflects Dalai Lama, the 'simple monk' and his straightforward message of world peace but is in stark contrast to the distortion of legibility. This disturbance shows the complexity of civilization and plays with the perception of the 'world peace message' being repeated time and again – losing its meaning and impact through millennia, centuries and decades.

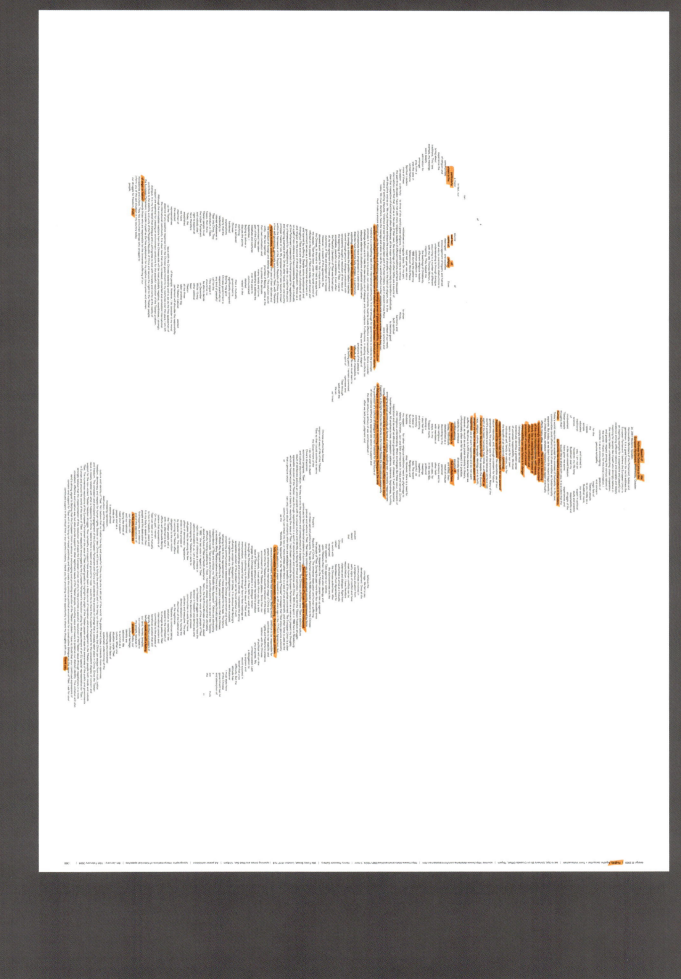

design © 2003 | Agatha Jacquelin + Tooni Voksander | lek et lo Kat, Unive's 55 on Casade Officet), 75gsm | source: http://www.dalailama.com/monthspeeches.htm | typographic representation for Autocraat speeches | 8th January 15th February 2004 | A2 poster exhibition | Bury Peacock Gallery | 39a Foley Street, London W1F 7LB | upising cross as Post Set, 12-8pm | 388 |

Alan Fletcher
I Have Nothing to Say
and I'm Saying It
John Cage: Lecture on
Nothing 1950

This is a short speech.

The self-portrait is of John Heartfield, an English name adopted by German Dadaist Helmuth Herzfelde (1891–1968). Here he is shown shouting provocative statements to irritate the Nazi party.

John Cage (1912–1992) was an American composer, poet, thinker, artist and an authority on mushrooms.

Alan Fletcher (1931–) stuck these bits together and chose yellow for the background. In the early 1960s he coaxed a printer in Sarzana, a small town in Liguria, to proof some of his wood letters. This typeface is one of them.

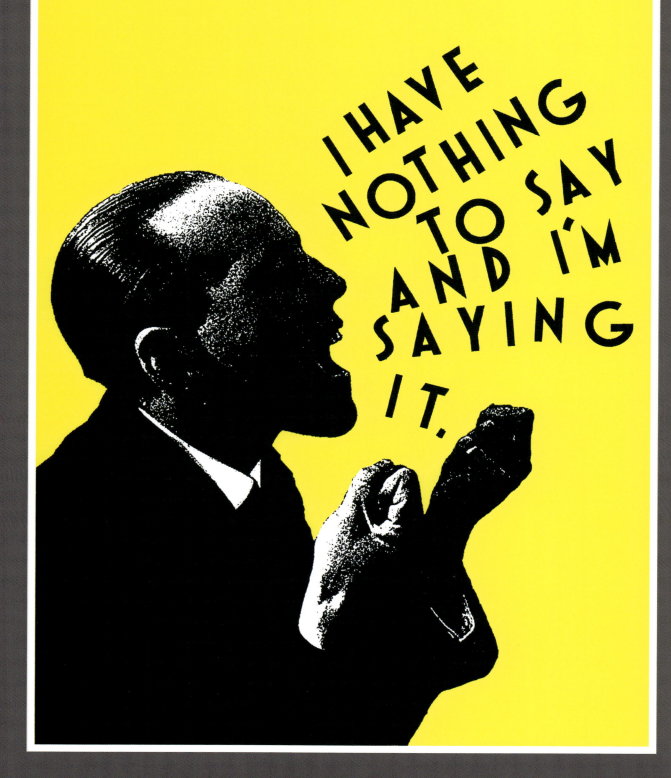

PHOTOGRAPH: JOHN HEARTFIELD. WORDS: JOHN CAGE. TYPEFACE: SARZANA. DESIGN: ALAN FLETCHER

Malcolm Frost

HG Wells: War of the Worlds, 1938 radio production by Orson Welles

"Attention all viewers, Orange Alert is now functioning.
Orange Alert! Orange Alert! Orange Alert!"

Herbert George Wells studied biology in 1886 and made his name in journalism after first trying to teach. Through connecting the everyday with the evidence of what he saw through his microscope and his huge literary imagination, HG Wells achieved fame with The Time Machine and War of the Worlds both published before the turn of the century.

George Orson Welles was an actor, producer, writer and director for radio, the stage and the cinema. With John Houseman, Welles founded the Mercury Theatre in 1937 and a year later produced the radio broadcast of War of the Worlds. The drama was so realistic that it caused panic in many parts of the States. The enhancement of the 'realism' was a direct result of the commercial breaks being interrupted by the fiction, and not as usual, the other way around.

The movie, directed by Byron Haskin in 1952, was the usual violent fantasy which failed as soon as the cardboard characters opened their mouths. Wells, Huxley, J G Ballard, Asimov, Arthur C Clarke, Michael Moorcock have been followed by dozens of youthful sci-fi writers, movie-makers, TV producers and so on; mainly because it's impossible to contain the vividness of our imaginations.

But the non-beeping Beagle 2 plus the current 'secret-war' alerts are testing our sense of human proportion to its limit (without our colourful fantasies working overtime, or indeed working at all).

"Keep vigilant at all times, but go about your daily activities freely. Orange alert!"
"Attention all passengers."

No one would have believed, in the last years of the nineteenth century, that human affairs were being watched keenly and closely by intelligences greater than man's and yet as mortal as his own; that as men busied themselves about their affairs they were scrutinized and studied, perhaps almost as narrowly as a man with a microscope might scrutinize the transient creatures that swarm and multiply in drops of water. ● With infinate complacency men went to and fro over this globe about their little affairs, serene in their assurance of their empire over matter. It is possible that the infusoria under the microscope do the same. No one gave a thought to the older worlds of space as sources of human danger, or thought to the older worlds of space as sources of human danger, or thought of them only to dismiss the idea of life upon them as impossible and improbable. It is curious to recall some of the mental habits of those departed days. At most, terrestrial men fancied there might be other men upon Mars, perhaps inferior to themselves and ready to welcome a missionary enterprise. Yet, across the gulf of space, minds that are to our minds as ours are to those of the beasts that perish, intellects vast and cool and unsympathetic, regarded this earth with envious eyes, and slowly and surely drew their plans against us. And early in the twentieth century came the great disillusionment. The planet Mars, I scarcely need remind listeners, revolves about the sun at a mean distance of 140,000,000 miles, and the light and heat it receives from the sun is barely half of that received by this world. It must be, if the nebular hypothesis has any truth, older than our world, and long before this earth ceased to be molten, life upon its surface must have begun its course. The fact that it is scarcely one-seventh of the volume of the earth must have accelerated its cooling to the temperature at which life could begin. It has air and water, and all that is necessary for the support of animated existence.

HG Wells 1898 | Orson Welles 1938 The War of The Worlds.
Poster Malcolm Frost | Igma London 2004

James Goggin

Using speech recognition; dictating text in Microsoft Office, Microsoft

My approach for the Public Address System poster was to concentrate on a literal interpretation of the show's premise: the translation of speech to typography.
I was initially drawn to the idea of mistakes that can occur during translation, but an unsuccessful search for examples where mistranslation had lead to an international incident within organisations such as the UN, somehow brought me to the Microsoft Office software manual.

"Say the following words to enter a sample sentence with a period at the end: 'You can dictate just about anywhere you can type (period)'"

This is an excerpt from the manual out-lining Office's speech recognition facility and shows one of the 'sample sentences' Microsoft asks the user to read aloud in order to 'train' the computer to under-stand their voice. While speech recognition software commonly mistranslates the user's voice, this specific sample sentence was itself of more interest to me and became the perfect 'speech' to use for my poster. It is perhaps not the kind of speech the exhibition curator intended, yet the line speaks somewhat loosely of the rela-tionship between the intangible voice and the tangible visual language that typo-graphy – the printed word – represents. Intrinsic to the sentence is the fact that it is written specifically to be read aloud – spoken – for translation from speech to text.

Displayed on the poster in Microsoft Word default Times New Roman, the sentence is ambiguous and has subtle political and linguistic connotations (the multiple mean-ings of the word 'dictate') and sounds strangely empowering. Take out the last line and you're left with a fairly accurate summary of recent superpower foreign policy: "You can dictate / just about any-where". It also sounds like an attempt at a definition of typography but slightly inarticulate, which seems odd coming from an authoritative source such as a manual.

The fact that this line is more or less writ-ten by Microsoft adds another layer of meaning, reading like a possible maxim for its business development model: just about anywhere you type (using Word), Microsoft can dictate.

You can dictate
just about anywhere
you can type.

Peter van der Gulden
and Przewalski ontwerpers
**Fear of Public Speaking
Clinic, America 2003**

Het slechte nieuws: ik heb mij verre
gehouden van Grote Woorden, uit vrees
mij uit te spreken. Het goede nieuws: ik
ga mijzelf van deze vrees verlossen.

The bad news: I kept myself from Big
Words, from anxiety of speaking out. The
good news: I'm going to release myself
from this fear.

The poster was set in Dialect roman and
Dialect open-face.

Type design & graphic design: Peter van der Gulden, www.przewalski.nl – Font: dialect roman & dialect titling – Text: www.changethatsrighthow.com/fear-of-public-speaking.asp & www.speech-writers.com/funerals.htm – Print: HAL, Zeefdruk, Elst, the Netherlands

EULOGY FOR MILITARY FUNERAL
Order our Ready-to-Go, eulogies for the death of an army person/officer. They are pre-written i.e. they are ready to be emailed to you, automatically, within 60 seconds of receiving your order. You will receive a set of short, alternative eulogies. Price: US$29.00 What do you receive?.Three eulogies, each one three minutes long. Suitable for: a comrad ⌐ officer of the ⌐

EULOGIES FO⌐
Eulogies or eu⌐ brother or siste⌐ emailed to you⌐ our receiving y⌐ ceive a selecti⌐ eulogies, any ⌐ used individua⌐ can choose, fr⌐ passages that ⌐ deceased. Plea⌐ for your order ⌐

EULOGIES FO⌐
Order our Rea⌐ sister. You may⌐ and-match the⌐ that best descr⌐ whom you are⌐ use in a church⌐ funeral home/⌐ crematorium ⌐ or graveside.⌐ Price: US$29.0⌐ What do you re⌐ Nine eulogies,⌐ three minutes⌐ passages from⌐ course create ⌐ Suitable for: s⌐ Sister or broth⌐ of deceased.⌐

FUNERAL REA⌐
Order our Rea⌐ ings. These rea⌐ mention of Go⌐ God or the afte⌐ afterlife but co⌐ church to com⌐ religious readi⌐ gospel extract⌐ provoking and⌐ meaningful fa⌐ farewell to sor⌐ someone spec⌐ Price: US$25.0⌐

FEAR OF PUBLIC SPEAKING GONE IN JUST 24 HOURS

It's official. FEAR OF PUBLIC SPEAKING is America's Greatest Fear – more feared than death itself. Jerry Seinfeld once joked that at a funeral, most people would rather in be in the casket than giving the eulogy! The good news is that our modern, fast, drug-free process will make you quickly feel completely different about public appearance, eliminating the fear so it never haunts you again.

If you are in business the cost of the fear of appearing in public is incalculable. Missed business opportunities. Passed over for promotion. This fear could cost you tens, even hundreds of thousands of dollars over your career. Now it will be gone for less than a round-trip business flight.

People's FEAR OF PUBLIC SPEAKING can be traced back to something like an incident at school where, when called upon by the teacher to speak, they were teased by other kids. When a person has a negative experience, the brain can link the negative feelings associated with that experience to other similar experiences. And so FEAR OF PUBLIC SPEAKING is born. Many people suffering from fear of public speaking believe that they are alone in feeling so frightened, but in fact it is shared by millions. The truth is that most people just don't want to talk about their fear of being in front of a group.

Called by many names – stage fright, speech anxiety, shyness, fear of speaking, performance anxiety, and speech phobia – FEAR OF PUBLIC SPEAKING can have a negative effect on careers and the ability to get things done. Symptoms may include shortness of breath, the inability to speak, a shaky voice, rapid breathing, rapid heartbeat, sweating, nausea etc.

The good news is that we will quickly and easily – even enjoyably – eliminate the fear so you can experience the joy and prestige and the career and social benefits of being totally relaxed in front of an audience. Working with us, you'll rapidly teach your unconscious mind to connect different, positive feelings to the stimuli that used to cause the FEAR OF PUBLIC SPEAKING. Its not hypnosis, but it is equally relaxing and enjoyable. Clients immediately notice that they feel different. Once your unconscious mind feels safe and knows now how to respond appropriately, you will always know – so the results are permanent. FEAR OF PUBLIC SPEAKING is gone. Forever.

Our FEAR OF PUBLIC SPEAKING Clinic is an entirely results-focused organization, so we charge you a flat rate of $987 for the result you want – freedom from FEAR OF PUBLIC SPEAKING. Commit 24 hours of your time and we guarantee you'll overcome your fear, or refund your fee.

David Hillman

**Everything You Always
Wanted to Know About Sex
(but were afraid to ask)
Woody Allen 1972**

"Is sex dirty? Only if it's done right."
I think it's a great quote… and it's true.

**Everything You Always
Wanted to Know About Sex
(but were afraid to ask)
Woody Allen 1972**

Is sex dirty? Only if it's done right. *Woody Allen*

Design: David Hillman, Pentagram

Everything you always wanted to know about sex (but were afraid to ask), 1972

Kim Hiorthøy
Me. We.
Muhammad Ali 1971

In 1967 Mohammad Ali refused induction by the US Army to go to war in Vietnam. His passport was taken, along with his championship title. His boxing licenses were cancelled and he was facing five years in prison. He did not box for two-and-a-half years. During this time he made money by speaking at universities and colleges. After giving a formal address at Harvard University, the students requested that Ali give a poem. He went back up and just said, "Me. We."

It may be difficult to understand fully what Mohammad Ali meant in America at that time – as a black person, as a boxer, as a speaker at an American university against the war – if you don't know the history. But that's not important. What he said still applies. Or it can, if we make it (and we should).

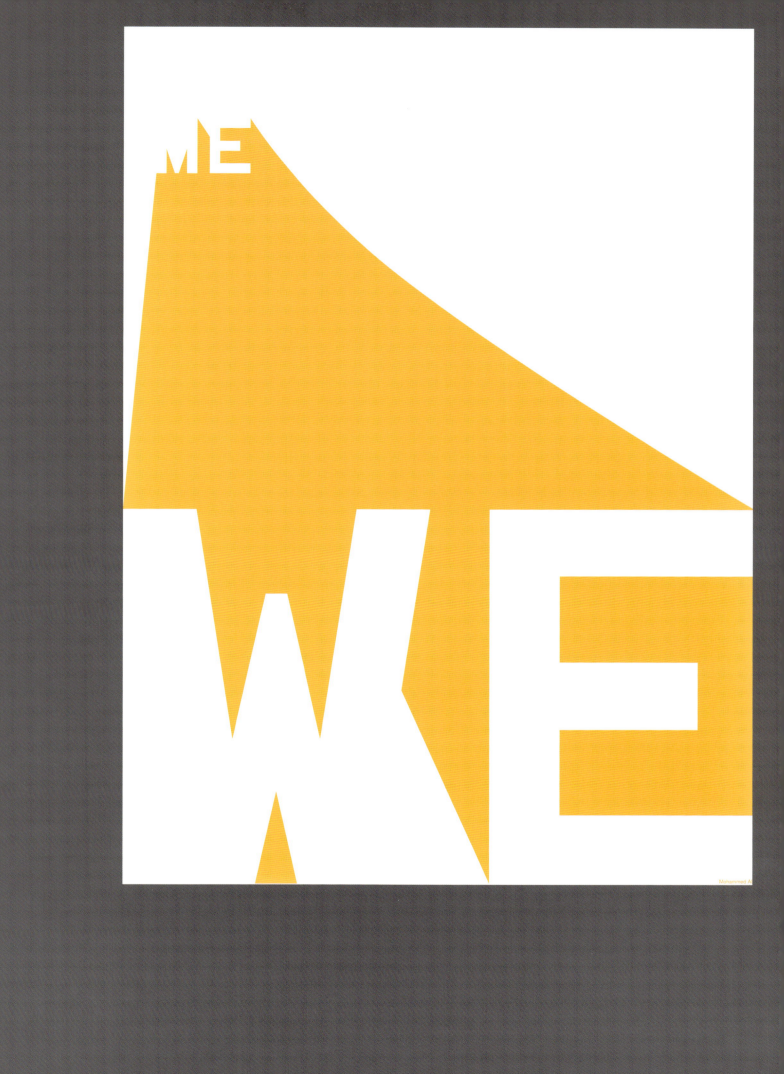

Angus Hyland

**I am the leaden army
that conquers the world;
I AM TYPE
Frederic Goudy 1927**

These quotes were collected to illustrate
the introduction of the third edition of
20th Century Type (Lewis Blackwell;
Laurence King Publishing, London 2004).
The main quote expresses the power of
the printed word.

It is not for the purpose of reviving old or making new rules that these facsimiles have been reproduced. One might as well try to provide models for unalterable fashions in garments, houses, furniture, or decoration. However pleasing a new fashion may be, that pleasure does not entirely suppress the desire for change, and that desire was never greater than it is now." / Less is more." Catalogues, posters, advertisements of all sorts. Believe me, they contain the poetry of our epoch. / Build a book like a body moving in space and time, like a dynamic relief in which every page is a surface carrying shapes, and every turn of a page a new crossing to a new stage of a single structure. / A photograph neither lies nor tells the truth." Colour is a creative element, not a trimming." The forms of the printed surface are taken in by seeing, not by

I AM THE LEADEN ARMY THAT CONQUERS THE WORLD: I AM TYPE

the more harmonious a letter, the more useful it is to reading. The more perfect and often exponent of form the artist's approach is of his own spiritual experience. / Typography must be as beautiful as its meaning form… Clarity is the essence of modern typography." / Contrast is the mark of our age." I am the leaden army that conquers the world: I AM TYPE. / All the old fellows stole our best ideas. / Type production has gone mad, with its senseless outpouring of new types… Only in degenerate times can 'Personality' (opposed to the nameless masses) become the aim of human development." / Contrast is perhaps the most important element in all modern design." / A layout man should be simple with good photographs. He should perform acrobatics when the pictures are bad. / Simplicity of form is never a poverty, it is a great virtue." / Art is a noun and design is a noun and also a verb." / Typography is an art, good typography is art. / Art in any form is a projected emotion using visual tools." / … a study of typography must include a study of the meaning of 'text'." Typography fostered the modern idea of individuality, but it destroyed the medieval sense of community and integration." Type can be a tool, a toy and a teacher." / Everything under the sun is art! / Communication should be entertaining." / You read best what you read most." / In order for language to function, signs must be isolable one from another (otherwise they would not be repeatable). At every level (phonetic, semantic, syntactic, and so on) language has its own laws of combination and continuity, but its primary material is constructed of irreducible atoms (phonemes for spoken language, and for written, signs…) … Language is a hierarchical combination of bits.

Theodore Low De Vinne / 1901
Ludwig Mies van der Rohe / 1912
Guillaume Apollinaire / 1913
El Lissitzky / 1920
John Heartfield / 1925
Piet Zwart / 1922
El Lissitzky / 1923
Piet Zwart / 1924
El Lissitzky / 1925
László Moholy-Nagy / 1926
Theo van Doesburg / 1926
Frederic Goudy / 1927
Frederic Goudy / Date unknown
Jan Tschichold / 1928
Jan Tschichold / 1928
Alexey Brodovitch / 1930
Jan Tschichold / 1930
Paul Rand / 1960
Paul Rand / 1960
Leslie Beall / 1964
Wolfgang Weingart / 1972
Neville Brody / 1989
Bradbury Thompson / 1986
Joseph Beuys / 1988
Neville Brody / 1991
Zuzana Licko / 1985
Yve-Alain Bois / 1997

12

Design by Pentagram. Printed by BAS Printers

Johnson Turnbull

The Nature of Readability from About Face: Reviving the Rules of Typography by David Jury, 2002

We are interested in the fact that written language and typography is essentially coded mark-making, but codes we are all familiar with. Its purpose, however, is not to obscure, but to reveal information.

Similarly, marks made by proof-readers in checking and correcting manuscripts are another, though more esoteric, form of coded information.

We wanted to create a poster that showed only these proofing marks, so we took an extract from the chapter The Nature of Readability in the book About Face: Reviving the Rules of Typography, by David Jury. We typed it out three times without using the delete key to correct any mistakes. The texts were then proof-read and the typed text stripped away, leaving only the skeleton of the proofing marks – a coding more akin to musical notation than type.

General

Search / replace double space

(errors in original marked on separate sheet)

Search / replace double spaces

Insert paragraph spaces ?

Remove word-breaks (worst cases only marked)

Errors in original marked on separate sheet

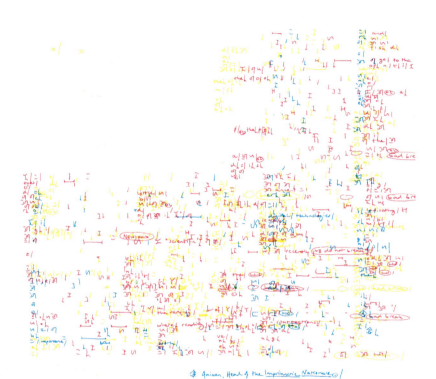

① Anisson, Head of the Imprimerie Nationale ⊙ /

② and the second in 'the Didot manner'

Creation date: 12 November 2003, Clerkenwell, London at a combined typing speed of 66.088 wpm.
ProofRead 13 November 2003, Chelsea, London.
Word Count: Total 2974 Unique 1542 Suspect 406
Documents:
<TypiEx Layout> Mon. Nov 3, 2003, 6.07PM

Alan Kitching
Address to Parliament
Winston Churchill 1940

The power of the spoken word and the human voice to move hearts and minds is awesome!

"Blood, toil, tears and sweat" was all Winston Churchill could offer the nation in his 13 May 1940 speech to the House of Commons following his appointment as Prime Minister. Nazi forces were conquering Europe and England seemed bound for defeat and occupation. Churchill's short, powerful words, expressed with gravitas, passion and pace, in his unique voice, exhorted all who heard to "wage war against a monstrous tyranny" and aim for "victory at all costs". This magical speech united the government and gave hope and new resolve to millions around the world.

The joy and challenge of this project for me was to translate, typographically, the magic and passion of this great orator's speech. It is not just the intensity of his words, but his pauses, stresses, tone and strength that make both visual and tangible something which originated in the mind and was expressed in air: an unseen, verbal text, a series of sounds.

The composition was printed letterpress from wood-letter. The final print is in an edition of ten copies.

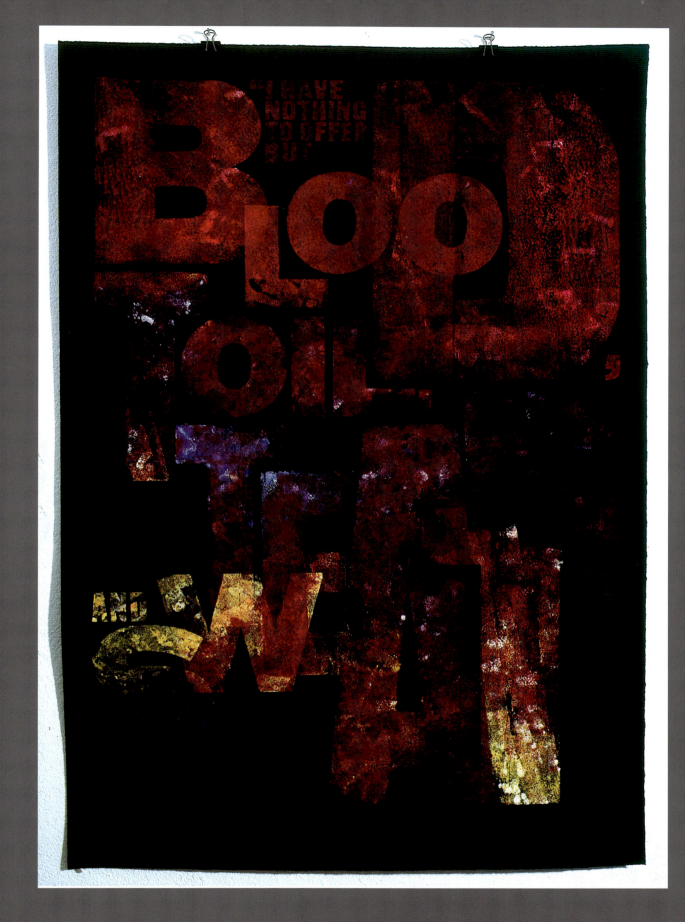

Christian Küsters

John Cage interviewed by Richard Kostelantz

Cage's ideal about society and art being without hierarchies has always appealed to me. No sound is greater than any other; in fact everything is music, as Cage demonstrated. Ultimately, he is as much about society as he is about art. Cage's work can be seen as being more philosophical, than being about the simple characteristics of a particular piece. I can relate to Cage's ideal of reducing the choices of the individual by setting up a system, and letting the system determine the final outcome. Within the boundaries set, the aesthetic becomes insignificant – a media to carry an idea. Cage wants us to look beyond the physical form of an exterior object and look at its internal 'motive'.

The poster is born of a system; the outcome is random within the boundaries set. The eye tracker visualises and objectifies the act of perception. The orange lines point at the retinal aspect of looking, a fundamental principle in art. It underlines an almost scientific perception of what the piece actually is, cutting out any judgment thus combining the two aspects of the system and the non-hierarchical perception.

THE HISTORY OF ART IS
SIMPLY A HISTORY OF
GETTING RID OF THE UGLY
BY ENTERING INTO IT, AND
USING IT. AFTER ALL, THE
NOTION OF SOMETHING
OUTSIDE OF US BEING UGLY
IS NOT OUTSIDE OF US BUT
INSIDE OF US. AND THAT'S
WHY I KEEP REITERATING
THAT WE ARE WORKING
WITH OUR MINDS. WHAT WE
ARE TRYING TO DO IS TO
GET THEM OPEN SO THAT
WE DO NOT SEE THINGS AS
BEING UGLY OR BEAUTIFUL
BUT WE SEE THEM JUST
AS THEY ARE. JOHN CAGE

Love
Response to US delegates upon their request for a signature on one of the first land treaties
Chief Wishham Fisherman

Our chosen speech was taken from 'Touch The Earth: A Self-Portrait Of Indian Existence', compiled by T C McLuhan, an Abacus book published by Sphere Books 1973.

A chief of one of the principal bands of the northern Blackfeet, upon being asked by US delegates for his signature to one of the first land treaties in his region of the Milk River, responds with a rejection of the money values of the white man.

"Our land is more valuable than your money. It will last forever. It will not even perish by the flames of fire. As long as the sun shines and the waters flow, this land will be here to give life to men and animals. We cannot sell the lives of men and animals; therefore we cannot sell this land. It was put here for us by the Great Spirit and we cannot sell it because it does not belong to us. You can count your money and burn it within the nod of a buffalo's head, but only the Great Spirit can count the grains of sand and the blades of grass of these plains. As a present to you, we will give you anything we have that you can take with you; but the land, never."

In choosing Native American culture in search of a quotation our aim was to refer to an attitude in history with longevity that still had a resonance today, while also avoiding the kind of sound bites that are forever selected for compendiums and school curricula.

The poignancy of such noble, simple words on the subject of self, nature, respect and spirituality against today's frenetic backdrop of capitalism, war and pollution is a reminder of the power and endurance of speech on a pure level and how it has become so misused. Our approach to the poster was to present the words in contrast to their alternative, where the inverse of the speaker's values are the commodities of life. The words are honest and said with conviction but are set either forced or broken with memorial-like overtones, succumbing to what we now know is the inevitable future and our reality.

The photography for the poster is by Amber Rowlands.

I t
will
last
foreve
r

It will not even perish by the flames of fire.
As long as the sun shines and the waters
flow, this land will be here to give life to
men and animals. We cannot sell the lives
of men and animals, therefore we cannot
sell this land. It was put here for us by the
Great Spirit and we cannot sell it because
it does not belong to us. You can count your
money and burn it within the nod of a
buffalo's head, but only the Great Spirit
can count the grains of sand and the blades
of grass of these plains. As a present to
you, we will give you anything we have
that you can take with you, but the land
forever.

**Culture 1991
Brian Eno: A Year With
Swollen Appendices:
The Diary of Brian Eno 1996**

When we were both students, we attended
a lecture given by Brian Eno at the Royal
College of Art. What struck us about his
talk (and subsequently his writing) was
Eno's clarity of thought – he tells you
nothing that you don't already know, but
simply puts new ideas or thoughts together
which make you think about things in an
unfamiliar way.

We make no pretence that this is the way
we always approach design, but in this
instance we simply enjoyed creating a bold,
juxtaposed typographic image that pos-
sesses a similar spirit to Eno's thoughts
and words.

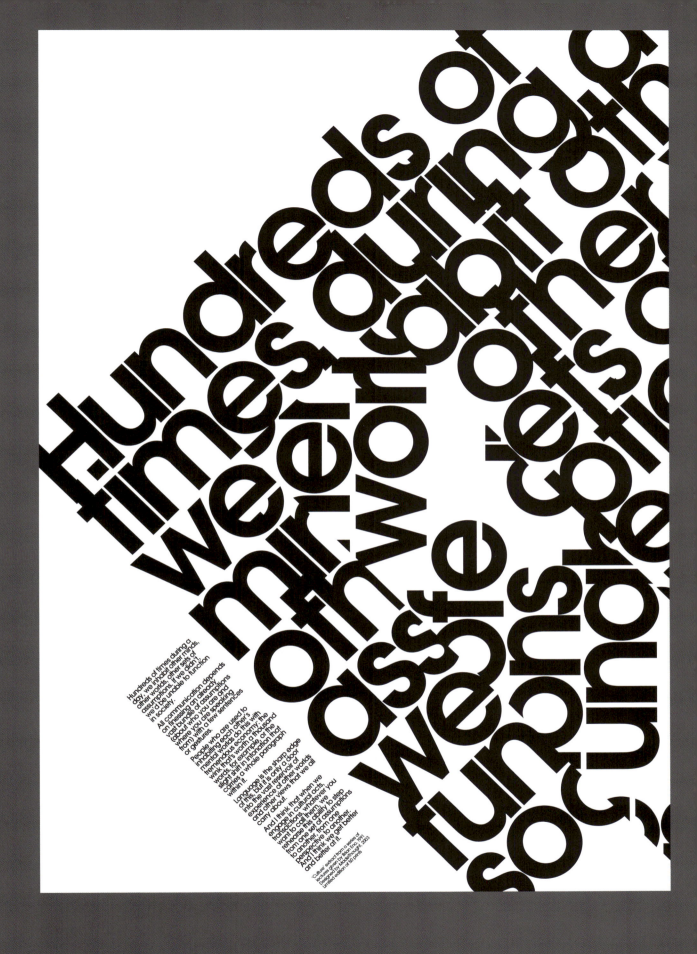

Hundreds of times during a day, we inhabit other worlds, other minds, other sets of assumptions. If we didn't, we'd be unable to function in society.

All communication depends on finessing all already vast bundle of assumptions (about who you are speaking from) with a few sentences or gestures.

People who are used to inhabiting each other's mental worlds do this with tremendous economy: the wink for example or the word, for example or the slight shift in information that carries a whole paragraph within it.

Language is the sharp edge of this, but it is only a door into the vast reservoir of experience of other worlds and other views that we all carry about.

And I think that when we engage in cultural acts, transactions, whatever you want to call them, we release this ability to step from one set of assumptions to another, from one perspective to another. And I think we get better and better at it.

'Cultural extract from a series of lectures given by Modern Eno, 1991
Designed by Modernhrough, 2003
Limited edition of 50 prints'

Marcus McCallion
Eric Gill 28 October 1934

The Libre Society (David Berry MA and myself) recently instigated a project that explores the idea of reflexive typography. Part of that research led me to revisit the writings of people like William Morris, John Ruskin and Eric Gill. I feel a lot of what they wrote and said is still significant to our society today, and particularly so when looking at the purpose of art, design and commerce.

I thought it would be interesting to utilise a speech by Gill, a typographer himself, who wrote passionately about social reform and the role of design and designers in creating a fairer society.

However, as much as I admire his work, I did not want this to be a sycophantic homage to an individual, but rather an interpretation of his ideas and ideals. For example, the poster does not use any of the typefaces designed by Gill himself, instead all the fonts have been drawn by myself and form part of the ÜNDT Foundry.

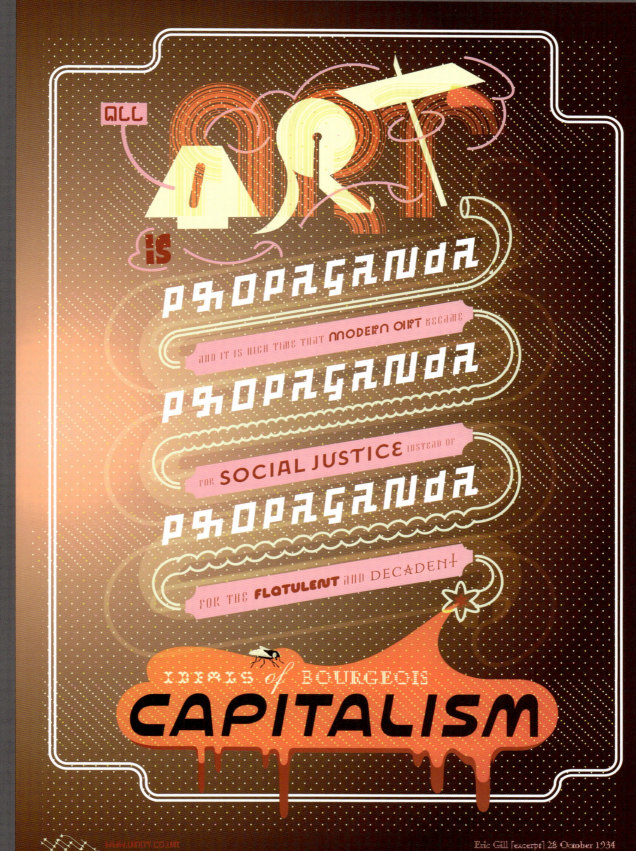

ALL ART is PROPAGANDA PROPAGANDA PROPAGANDA and it is high time that MODERN ART became for SOCIAL JUSTICE instead of for the FLATULENT and DECADENT IDEALS of BOURGEOIS CAPITALISM

www.uniqt.co.uk

Eric Gill [excerpt] 28 October 1934

Michael Morrisoe
**In Event of Moon Disaster:
speech written for President
Nixon by Bill Safire
18 July 1969**

The design of the poster is a metaphor
for the speech it interprets. The speech in
question was one written for President
Nixon two days before Neil Armstrong and
Buzz Aldrin set foot on the moon. As legend
goes, the good people at NASA were sure of
most things going according to plan on the
mission, but they had no idea at all if the
moon-landing vehicle would be able to set
back off from the moon. In the event of the
astronauts being stranded on the moon
Bill Safire (Nixon's speech writer) prepared
a speech entitled In Event of Moon Disaster,
which could be used immediately if the
astronauts should get into trouble.

When I read the speech it made me appreciate the power of such speeches in
comparison to those spoken. It made me
question if speeches change history, or
simply react to it. It also set me thinking
about what other contingency speeches
had been prepared.

The speech is displayed on the metal plate
in order to suggest it never having been
printed, as the words were never actually
spoken.

To: H.R. Haldeman
From: Bill Safire

July 18, 1969

IN EVENT OF MOON DISASTER:

Fate has ordained that the men who went to the
moon to explore in peace will stay there and rest in peace.
These brave men, Neil Armstrong and Edwin
Aldrin, know that there is no hope for their recovery. But
they also know that there is hope for mankind in their sacrifice.

These two men are laying down their lives in
mankinds most noble goal: the search for truth and understanding.

They will be mourned by their families and
friends; they will be mourned by their nation; they will be
mourned by the people of the world;they will be mourned by
a mother earth that dared send two of her sons into the
unknown.

In their exploration, they stirred the people of
the world to feel as ones in their sacrifice, they bind
more tightly the brotherhood of man.

In ancient days, men looked at stars and saw
their heroes in constellations. In modern times, we do much
the same, but our heroes are epic men of flesh and blood.

Others will follow, and surely find their way
home. Mans search will not be denied. But these men were
the first, and they will remain the foremost in our hearts.

For every human being who looks up at the moon
in the nights to come will know that there is some corner
of another world that is forever mankind.

PRIOR TO THE PRESIDENTS STATEMENT:

The president should telephone each of the wid-
ows-to-be.

AFTER THE PRESIDENTS STATEMENT, AT THE POINT WHEN NASA ENDS
COMMUNICATION WITH THE MEN:

A clergyman should adopt the same procedure as a
burial at sea, commending their souls to the deepest of the
deep, concluding with the lords prayer.

Morag Myerscough

Replacing speech: two years worth of text messages 2002–03

Over the last two years I have been collecting all the text messages I receive. Text messages as a form of speech fascinate me because they are concise and have to be thought about carefully before being executed. They're also a very discreet way of communicating and usually you can recognise the person who texts you from the way they write. It's a very personal exchange and almost romantic, like a love letter. Texts can often be more intimate than actually talking to someone and now replace a lot of face-to-face conversations.

This poster records some of the text messages I have received in the last two years. The texts I sent were not so important but just from revisiting those I received I can remember the moment exactly. Recording memories is very important to me, especially because there is a tendency now to continually experience new things but not to commit them to memory. Even though texts are very immediate and transitory, recording these conversations forms a lasting memento of my experiences.

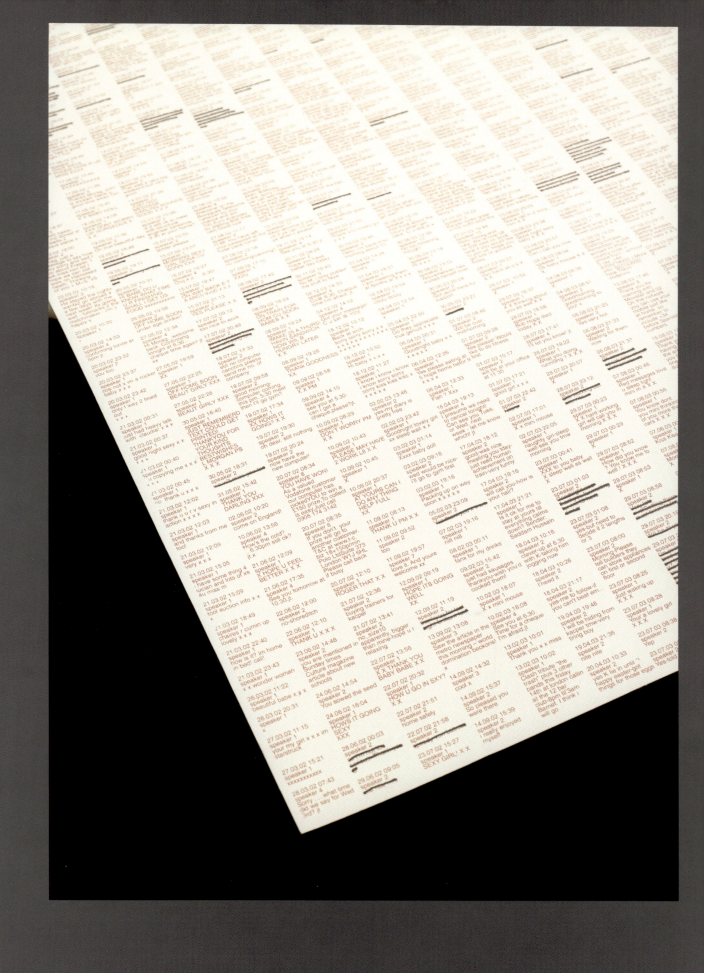

Naked Design
Speech to the commanders of the troops responsible for enforcing martial law in Beijing, Deng Xiaoping 1989

In 1989 I was living in Hong Kong, happily travelling into China, making friends, living the life of Riley when the events unfolded. Up until the tanks rolled in there had been an air of optimism politically. Attempts by people in Hong Kong to get in touch with their kin on the mainland were rebuffed by those relatives themselves for fear of arrest. Rumours on the 'Million Man March' in Hong Kong that summer included the use of methamphetamine injections on the soldiers of the PLA, which brought on a drug-based psychosis and exacerbated the massacre.

Deng Xiaoping went on to point out that western governments had adopted similar behaviour in the past and would go on to do so again.

}} PLA }}}

All in, all, this was a test, and we passed

Deng Xiaoping

In the springtime of 1989, less than four months after Palestinians had shaken off their acquiescence to Israeli occupation and launched the intifada, the students of Beijing moved suddenly to the centre of the World's attention demanding democracy for China.

The demonstration occurred on April 22 whilst the students were also out celebrating the remembrance of a national hero.

On June 4, 1989, Deng Xiaoping, the then Chinese leader, ordered troops to disperse the demonstration in Tiananmen Square which resulted in a massacre of citizenry. On the same day in Poland Solidarity won a huge majority of the vote.

Five days after Deng Xiaoping, spoke to the commanders of the troops who were responsible for enforcing martial law in Beijing.

Five months later on Thursday, the 9th of November 1989 the Berlin Wall fell.

Comrades, you have been working hard. First of all, I'd like to express my heartfelt condolences to the comrades in the People's Liberation Army, the armed police, and police who died in the struggle — and my sincere sympathy and solicitude to the comrades in the army, the armed police, and the police who were wounded in the struggle, and I want to extend my sincere regards to all the army, armed police, and police personnel who participated in the struggle.

I suggest that all of us stand and pay a silent tribute to the martyrs.

I'd like to take this opportunity to say a few words. This storm was bound to arrive sooner or later. As determined by the international macro-climate and the domestic micro-climate, it was bound to happen and was independent of man's will. It was just a matter of time and scale of the storm. It has turned out in our favour, for we still have a huge group of veterans who have experienced many storms and have a thorough understanding of things. They were on the side of taking resolute action to counter the turmoil. Although some comrades may not understand this now, they will understand eventually and will support the decision of the Central Committee.

The 26 April editorial of the People's Daily classified the problem as turmoil. The word was appropriate, but some people objected to the word and tried to amend it. But what has happened shows that this verdict was right. It was also inevitable that the turmoil would develop into a counter-revolutionary rebellion.

We still have a group of senior comrades who are alive, we still have the army, and we also have a group of core cadres who took part in the revolution at various times. That is why it was relatively easy for us to handle the present matter. The main difficulty in handling this matter lay in that we had never experienced such a situation before, in which a small minority of bad people mixed with so many young students and onlookers. We did not have a clear picture of the situation, and this prevented us from taking some actions that we should have taken earlier.

It would have been difficult for us to understand the nature of the matter had we not had the support of so many senior comrades. Some comrades do not understand the nature of the problem. They think it is simply a question of how to treat the masses. Actually, what we face is not simply ordinary people who are unable to distinguish between right and wrong. We also face a rebellious clique and a large number of the **dregs of society** who want to topple our country and overthrow our party. This is the essence of the problem. Failing to understand this fundamental issue means failing to understand the nature of the incident. I believe that after serious work, we can win the support of the overwhelming majority of comrades within the party concerning the nature of the incident and its handling.

The incident became very clear as soon as it broke out. They have two main slogans. One is to topple the Communist Party, and the other is to overthrow the socialist system. Their goal is to establish a totally Western-dependent bourgeois republic. The people want to combat corruption. This, of course, we accept. We should also take the so-called anticorruption slogans raised by people with ulterior motives as good advice and accept them accordingly. Of course, these slogans are just a front. The heart of these slogans is to topple the Communist Party and overthrow the socialist system.

In the course of quelling this rebellion, many of our comrades were injured or even sacrificed their lives. Their weapons were also taken from them. Why was this? It also was because bad people mingled with the good, which made it difficult to take the drastic measures we should take.

Handling this matter amounted to a very severe political test for our army, and what happened shows that our PLA passed muster. If we had used tanks to roll across bodies, it would have created a confusion of fact and fiction across the country. That is why I have to thank the PLA commanders and fighters for using this attitude to deal with the rebellion. Even though the losses are regrettable, this has enabled us to win over the people and made it possible for those people who can't tell right from wrong to change their viewpoint. This has made it possible for everyone to see for themselves what kind of people the PLA are, whether there was bloodshed at Tiananmen, and who were the people who shed blood.

Once this question is cleared up, we can seize the initiative. Although it is very saddening to have sacrificed so many comrades, if the course of the incident is analysed objectively, people cannot but recognize that the PLA are the sons and brothers of the people. This will also help the people to understand the measures we used in the course of the struggle. In the future, the PLA will have the people's support for whatever measures it takes to deal with whatever problem it faces. I would like to add here that in the future we must never again let people take away our weapons. All in all, this was a test, and we passed.

Justus Oehler

Ich bin ein Berliner
John F Kennedy, Rudolph
Wilde Platz, West Berlin
26 June 1963

I tried to visualise how of some speeches we remember but a few words, which have become a symbol for that speech. The rest of the speech, however, we have probably never even read or heard. Hence on the poster the actual speech of JFK is set as a solid block (hard to read), with the final sentence 'extracted' in red.

Justus Oehler
Ich bin ein Berliner
John F Kennedy, Rudolph
Wilde Platz, West Berlin
26 June 1963

I AM PROUD TO COME TO THIS CITY AS THE GUEST OF YOUR DISTINGUISHED MAYOR, WHO HAS SYMBOLIZED THROUGHOUT THE WORLD THE FIGHTING SPIRIT OF WEST BERLIN. AND I AM PROUD TO VISIT THE FEDERAL REPUBLIC WITH YOUR DISTINGUISHED CHANCELLOR WHO FOR SO MANY YEARS HAS COMMITTED GERMANY TO DEMOCRACY AND FREEDOM AND PROGRESS, AND TO COME HERE IN THE COMPANY OF MY FELLOW AMERICAN, GENERAL CLAY, WHO HAS BEEN IN THIS CITY DURING ITS GREAT MOMENTS OF CRISIS AND WILL COME AGAIN IF EVER NEEDED. TWO THOUSAND YEARS AGO THE PROUDEST BOAST WAS "CIVIS ROMANUS SUM." TODAY, IN THE WORLD OF FREEDOM, THE PROUDEST BOAST IS "ICH BIN EIN BERLINER." I APPRECIATE MY INTERPRETER TRANSLATING MY GERMAN! THERE ARE MANY PEOPLE IN THE WORLD WHO REALLY DON'T UNDERSTAND, OR SAY THEY DON'T, WHAT IS THE GREAT ISSUE BETWEEN THE FREE WORLD AND THE COMMUNIST WORLD. LET THEM COME TO BERLIN. THERE ARE SOME WHO SAY THAT COMMUNISM IS THE WAVE OF THE FUTURE. LET THEM COME TO BERLIN. AND THERE ARE SOME WHO SAY IN EUROPE AND ELSEWHERE WE CAN WORK WITH THE COMMUNISTS. LET THEM COME TO BERLIN. AND THERE ARE EVEN A FEW WHO SAY THAT IT IS TRUE THAT COMMUNISM IS AN EVIL SYSTEM, BUT IT PERMITS US TO MAKE ECONOMIC PROGRESS. LASS' SIE NACH BERLIN KOMMEN. LET THEM COME TO BERLIN. FREEDOM HAS MANY DIFFICULTIES AND DEMOCRACY IS NOT PERFECT, BUT WE HAVE NEVER HAD TO PUT A WALL UP TO KEEP OUR PEOPLE IN, TO PREVENT THEM FROM LEAVING US. I WANT TO SAY ON BEHALF OF MY COUNTRYMEN, WHO LIVE MANY MILES AWAY ON THE OTHER SIDE OF THE ATLANTIC WHO ARE FAR DISTANT FROM YOU, THAT THEY TAKE THE GREATEST PRIDE THAT THEY HAVE BEEN ABLE TO SHARE WITH YOU, EVEN FROM A DISTANCE, THE STORY OF THE LAST 18 YEARS. I KNOW OF NO TOWN, NO CITY, THAT HAS BEEN BESIEGED FOR 18 YEARS THAT STILL LIVES WITH THE VITALITY AND THE FORCE, AND THE HOPE AND THE DETERMINATION OF THE CITY OF WEST BERLIN. WHILE THE WALL IS THE MOST OBVIOUS AND VIVID DEMONSTRATION OF THE FAILURES OF THE COMMUNIST SYSTEM, FOR ALL THE WORLD TO SEE, WE TAKE NO SATISFACTION IN IT, FOR IT IS, AS YOUR MAYOR HAS SAID, AN OFFENSE NOT ONLY AGAINST HISTORY BUT AN OFFENSE AGAINST HUMANITY, SEPARATING FAMILIES, DIVIDING HUSBANDS AND WIVES AND BROTHERS AND SISTERS, AND DIVIDING A PEOPLE WHO WISH TO BE JOINED TOGETHER. WHAT IS TRUE OF THIS CITY IS TRUE OF GERMANY - REAL, LASTING PEACE IN EUROPE CAN NEVER BE ASSURED AS LONG AS ONE GERMAN OUT OF FOUR IS DENIED THE ELEMENTARY RIGHT OF FREE MEN, AND THAT IS TO MAKE A FREE CHOICE. IN 18 YEARS OF PEACE AND GOOD FAITH, THIS GENERATION OF GERMANS HAS EARNED THE RIGHT TO BE FREE, INCLUDING THE RIGHT TO UNITE THEIR FAMILIES AND THEIR NATION IN LASTING PEACE WITH GOOD WILL TO ALL PEOPLE. YOU LIVE IN A DEFENDED ISLAND OF FREEDOM, BUT YOUR LIFE IS PART OF THE MAIN. SO LET ME ASK YOU, AS I CLOSE, TO LIFT YOUR EYES BEYOND THE DANGERS OF TODAY, TO THE HOPES OF TOMORROW, BEYOND THE FREEDOM MERELY OF THIS CITY OF BERLIN, OR YOUR COUNTRY OF GERMANY, TO THE ADVANCE OF FREEDOM EVERYWHERE, BEYOND THE WALL TO THE DAY OF PEACE WITH JUSTICE, BEYOND YOURSELVES AND OURSELVES TO ALL MANKIND. FREEDOM IS INDIVISIBLE, AND WHEN ONE MAN IS ENSLAVED, ALL ARE NOT FREE. WHEN ALL ARE FREE THEN WE CAN LOOK FORWARD TO THAT DAY WHEN THIS CITY WILL BE JOINED AS ONE AND THIS COUNTRY AND THIS GREAT CONTINENT OF EUROPE IN A PEACEFUL AND HOPEFUL GLOBE. WHEN THAT DAY FINALLY COMES, AS IT WILL, THE PEOPLE OF WEST BERLIN CAN TAKE SOBER SATISFACTION IN THE FACT THAT THEY WERE IN THE FRONT LINES FOR ALMOST TWO DECADES. ALL FREE MEN, WHEREVER THEY MAY LIVE, ARE CITIZENS OF BERLIN, AND, THEREFORE, AS A FREE MAN, I TAKE PRIDE IN THE WORDS

"ICH BIN EIN BERLINER"

Michael C Place
Speech from lunar orbit
US Astronaut Frank Borman
24 December 1968

[static].
[pause].

Hand-drawn [by MCP] using Staedler Permanent Lumocolor pens B/M/F [Black], Staedler Pigment Liner 07, Pilot Drawing Pen, Pentel Permanent Marker [B] on A1 folded into A2 [1,5 + 10mm] gridded graph paper [manufacturer unknown]. [Black marker] Space as a metaphor for Heaven, Frank Borman's speech from Apollo 8 draws from the Bible a very un-space/NASA[tm]-like communication [incomplete without static] of peace and goodwill to the good people of the Earth. Hand lettered small type [see top] invokes the very personal speech from Earth's lunar orbit, the large block of black space implies the us/them blankness of space/distance.

[static].
[pause].

Indicators [see left of poster] showing where markers ran out are suggestive of the stages [booster rockets/main stage etc.] of putting man into space. The piece was done by hand [no computer was used] and harks back to a more idyllic time of hand-written letters. I see Frank Borman's communication essentially as a letter home.

[static]...

(STATIC)... AND GOD SAID "LET THE WATERS UNDER THE HEAVEN BE GATHERED INTO ONE PLACE.
(PAUSE) AND LET THE DRY LANDS APPEAR AND IT WAS SO (PAUSE) AND GOD CALLED THE DRY LAND EARTH
(PAUSE) AND THE GATHERING TOGETHER OF THE WATERS CALLED THESE SEAS
(PAUSE) AND GOD SAW THAT IT WAS GOOD.
(STATIC)... AND FROM THE CREW OF APOLLO 8 (PAUSE) WE CALL FOR GOODNIGHT (PAUSE) GOOD LUCK (PAUSE) A MERRY CHRISTMAS AND GOD BLESS ALL OF YOU
(PAUSE) ALL OF YOU ON THE GOOD EARTH.
(STATIC)...

David Quay
Painting Speech, William Massey, 17th-century poet

"Whence did the wond'rous mystic art arise,
Of painting SPEECH, and speaking to the eyes?
That we by tracing magic lines are taught,
How to embody, and to colour THOUGHT?"
—William Massey

This typographic fusion of two of The Foundry's fonts combines the 'traditional' contours of Foundry Wilson, with the experimental digital approach of Foundry Flek in a juxtaposition where magic lines meet.

The quote chosen was a gift. While deciding what to interpret typographically, a student, who we have been advising on a typography project, came to the studio clutching his 'find of the year' from a South Bank bookstall – A Book of Scripts by Alfred Fairbank, King Penguin Edition (48), Tschichold-styled paperback, first published in 1949. The quote appears as the opener to the body of the text. For us these words encapsulate typography, a powerful tool that evokes so much – we have not come across a more expressive description than "painting speech".

Something of an enigma, we could find nothing about the man behind the words, believed to be William Massey. We think he lived in the late 17th century, was maybe American, possibly Quaker. The quote was used in an 1828 needlework sampler, but it has also been attributed to Marshall McLuhan! The mystery adds a frisson to the words. If anyone knows more please let us know.

Whence did the wond'rous
mystic art arise,
Of painting SPEECH,
and speaking to the eyes?
That we by tracing magic
lines are taught,
How to embody, and to
colour THOUGHT?

WILLIAM MASSEY

Design: David Quay/The Foundry

Two speeches delivered on 19 March 2003, two days before the Iraq conflict; the first by British Commander Tim Collins, the second by American Vice Admiral Timothy Keating

The differing approaches of the UK and US to rouse their troops before the recent Iraq conflict struck us immediately upon receiving the round-robin email that inspired this poster. At first we were attracted by its comic value, but on reflection the reality is more disturbing.

We're cynical enough to realise that the speeches were carefully thought-out propaganda, crafted to package the impending war to uncertain populations back home. What is interesting is the different ways the two allies chose to present this.

We tried to draw upon the appropriate typographic reference material when pre-senting the two approaches. The British commanding officer exploited a tradition of troop-rousing addresses from a time when war was thought of as noble and necessary for the greater good to prevail. He wanted to occupy a moral high ground. His US equivalent went for a crass CNN/MTV-friendly sound bite with a side of action movie bravado to engender some patriotic spirit in the troops and population.

We suppose the US approach was a more honest representation of the reasons behind the war in Iraq but perhaps we prefer to have the wool pulled over our eyes in a more eloquent, intellectual manner. Hell, for a moment back there we almost believed Colonel Tim Collins!

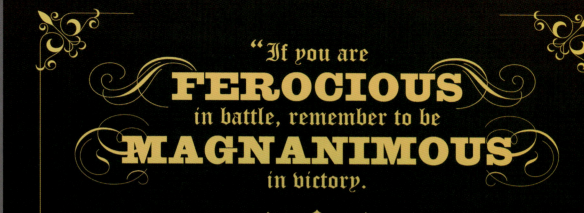

"If you are **FEROCIOUS** in battle, remember to be **MAGNANIMOUS** in victory.

We go to liberate, not to conquer. We are entering Iraq to free a people, and the only flag that will be flown in that ancient land is their own.

Don't treat them as refugees, for they are in their own country.

"Make no mistake, when the president says go - look out, it's hammer time."

U.S. Vice Admiral Timothy Keating

On board USS Constellation on the eve of war with Iraq, to the strains of Queen's 'We Will Rock You'.

properly and mark their graves.

You will be shunned unless your conduct is of the highest, for your deeds will follow you down history. Iraq is steeped in history. It is the site of the Garden of Eden, of the Great Flood and the birth of Abraham.

TREAD LIGHTLY THERE"

Excerpts from the address of Lieutenant Colonel Tim Collins to the 1st Battalion of the Royal Irish

~ MARCH 19TH 2003 ~

Kev Rice and Dave Smith
**The Woyzeck Wound: speech
written for Nelson Mandela
on receiving the 1985 Büchner
Prize in Darmstadt
Heiner Müller 1985**

The speech we have chosen has a fragmentary quality that we both like. As artists and curators much of what we do is collaborative, whether between ourselves or with other artists. Our intention with this poster was to put heterogeneous elements together and instigate some sort of compromising of the autonomy of each individual part, making their respective functions subservient to the experience of the whole piece. We want to acknowledge through the micro-version of this poster, that interaction between disparate artworks is inevitable because they are not mutually exclusive of each other or the wider context in which they exist. Making art is much the same as looking at it. The viewer, her/his environment and all artworks hitherto experienced have an effect on the viewed art object. We are interested in the process of making art, rather than expressing a deliberate message or meaning. The process of making art is like mixing colours. Like colour, visual language already exists. The important thing is that what we do forms part of an experience.

Kev Rice and Dave Smith
**The Woyzeck Wound: speech
written for Nelson Mandela
on receiving the 1985 Büchner
Prize in Darmstadt
Heiner Müller 1985**

THE WOYZECK WOUND

THRONG

Still Woyzeck shaves his captain, eats his prescribed peas, tortures Marie ... his population turned into a state, surrounded by ghosts: the Fusilier Runge plays his blood-stained brother, proletarian tool of Rosa Luxemburg's killers; his prison is called Stalingrad where he is faced with the murdered Marie in a Kriemhild mask; her statue stands on Mamaishill, her German memorial: the iron curtain, in Berlin, the convoy of armoured tanks of the revolution, coagulated to politics. HIS MOUTH PRESSED ONTO THE SHOULDER OF THE OFFICER KEEPING THE PEACE WHO LEADS HIM OFF LIGHT-FOOTED is how Kafka saw him disappear from the stage, after the murder of his brother ALL THE TIME STRUGGLING TO KEEP DOWN HIS FINAL NAUSEA. Or as a patient whose doctor is laid in his bed, with the wound open like a coal seam ... Goya's giant was his first appearance, sitting on the mountains, counting the years of tyranny, father of guerillas. On a mural in a cell of a monastery in Parma I saw his severed feet, gigantic in an Arcadian landscape. Somewhere, his body is swinging itself along, perhaps on its hands, perhaps shaking with laughter, into an unknown future which could be his interbreeding with the machine, thrust up against the force of gravity in the jetstream of rockets. In Africa he still sets out on his crusade into history; time is not on his side any more, and his hunger, too, is perhaps not a revolutionary element any more, now it can be stilled with bombs, while the drum majors of the world devastate the planet, the battlefield of tourists, the first-strike runway, no eyes for the fire that the infantry soldier Franz Johann Christoph Woyzeck, whittling sticks for the running of the gauntlet, saw spreading across the skies in Darmstadt, Ulrike Meinhof, Prussia's daughter and late-born bride of another of German literature's foundlings who buried himself at Wannsee, she, protagonist in the last drama of the bourgeois world, of the RETURN OF THE YOUNG COMRADE OUT OF THE LIMESTONE QUARRY now armed to his teeth, she, his sister wearing Marie's bloody necklace.

HEINER FOR MULLER

3

THE HEINE WOUND begins to scar, crooked, WOYZECK is the open wound. Woyzeck lives where the dog is buried, with the nigger to the woodpit, the dog/the nigger is the hope of the dog/nigger. For his incarnation we wait in fear and/or hope of the dog/nigger to return as a wolf. The wolf that comes from the south. When the sun stands at its zenith, he is at one with our shadow, then, in the hour of mean-destroyer, history begins. Not until history has happened is the collective extinction in the frost of entropy worthwhile, or, cut short by politics, in the big bang that will be the end of all utopias and the beginning of a reality beyond mankind.

2

A text, many times abused by the theatre, that happened to a twenty-three year old who has had his eyelids snipped off at birth by the Fates, torn apart by fever into orthographic snillcrosce, a motif that might emerge a future-riddling as the hand holding the spoon trembles at the sight of the future, blocking the gates to paradise as an insomniac angel, where the innocence of playwriting was once at home. How harmless the crown of modern drama, Beckett's Waiting for Godot next to this quick thunderstorm approaching at the speed of another age, Lenz packed in his bags, the lightning doused in Lvouis, the age of George Heym in the place with no utopia underneath the ice blanket in the Havel, Konrad Bayer in the disembowelled skull of Vitus Bering, Rolf-Dieter Brinkmann looking left in the right-hand lane in front of SHAKESPEARE'S PUB, hos shameless the lof of the POSTHISTOIRE next to the barbaric reality of our pre-history.

LOVE OF HIS

NELSON MANDELA

Erik Spiekermann

The Awful German Language
Mark Twain: A Tramp Abroad
1880

I chose the speech by Mark Twain because all my other favourite speeches would have been in German, and thus no good to an audience in London. This excerpt comes from Twain's essay "The awful German Language" and, while large chunks of it are in what he considers to be German, it is still comprehensible to an audience who doesn't speak my language. It uses the prejudice you all have about us, the Krauts. Our language shows that, indeed, we are a nation of mechanically minded perfectionists. And then again, we're not. The ability to laugh about ourselves is not too highly developed, but I certainly understand Twain's frustration with that awful language of ours. But at least he went there, learnt it and thus understands that a culture can only be appreciated through its language. How can anybody who doesn't speak or understand the language say that Germans have no sense of humour? If we did, he wouldn't know.

The poster designed itself: the English text is set in Caslon, the typeface that George Bernard Shaw always specified for his writings; the German copy is set in Fraktur, the typeface used for setting German and other northern languages since Gutenberg.

If it hadn't been for the Nazis misusing these faces for their sinister purposes, we would still be reading Fraktur. It is the typeface of Goethe, Martin Luther, Karl Marx and Hegel. And it is perfectly suited to set our long words and interminable sentences, still evoking Gothic cathedrals and narrow streets with timbered houses. The one used is called Wittenberg Fraktur, after the town where Luther nailed his theses on a church door in 1517.

A Fourth of July Oration in the German Tongue, Delivered at a Banquet of the Anglo-American Club of Students by the Author of this Book.

~~~

GENTLEMEN: Since I arrived, a month ago, in this old wonderland, this vast garden of Germany, my English tongue has so often proved a useless piece of baggage to me, and so troublesome to carry around, in a country where they haven't the checking system for luggage, that I finally set to work, last week, and learned the German language. Also! Es freut mich daß dies so ist, denn es muß, in ein hauptsächlich degree, höflich sein, daß man auf ein occasion like this, sein Rede in die Sprache des Landes worin he boards, aussprechen soll. Dafür habe ich, aus reinische Verlegenheit – no, Vergangenheit – no, I mean Höflichkeit – aus reinische Höflichkeit habe ich resolved to tackle this business in the German language, um Gottes willen! Also! Sie müssen so freundlich sein, und verzeih mich die interlarding von ein oder zwei Englischer Worte, hie und da, denn ich finde daß die deutsche is not a very copious language, and so when you've really got anything to say, you've got to draw on a language that can stand the strain.

Wenn aber man kann nicht meinem Rede verstehen, so werde ich ihm später dasselbe übersetz, wenn er solche Dienst verlangen wollen haben werden sollen sein hätte. (I don't know what wollen haben werden sollen sein hätte means, but I notice they always put it at the end of a German sentence – merely for general literary gorgeousness, I suppose.)

This is a great and justly honored day – a day which is worthy of the veneration in which it is held by the true patriots of all climes and nationalities – a day which offers a fruitful theme for thought and speech; und meinem Freunde – no, meinen Freunden – meines Freundes – well, take your choice, they're all the same price; I don't know which one is right – also! ich habe gehabt haben worden gewesen sein, as Goethe says in his *Paradise Lost* – ich – ich – that is to say – ich – but let us change cars.

Also! Die Anblick so viele Großbrittanischer und Amerikanischer hier zusammengetroffen in Brüderliche concord, ist zwar a welcome and inspiriting spectacle. And what has moved you to it? Can the terse German tongue rise to the expression of this impulse? Is it Freundschaftsbezeigungenstadtverordnetenversammlungenfamilieneigenthümlichkeiten? Nein, o nein! This is a crisp and noble word, but it fails to pierce the marrow of the impulse which has gathered this friendly meeting and produced diese Anblick – eine Anblick welche ist gut zu sehen – gut für die Augen in a foreign land and a far country – eine Anblick solche als in die gewöhnliche Heidelberger phrase nennt man ein »schönes Aussicht!« Ja, freilich natürlich wahrscheinlich ebensowohl! Also! Die Aussicht auf dem Königsstuhl mehr größerer ist, aber geistliche sprechend nicht so schön, lob' Gott! Because sie sind hier zusammengetroffen, in Brüderlichem concord, ein großen Tag zu feiern, whose high benefits were not for one land and one locality only, but have conferred a measure of good upon all lands that know liberty to-day, and love it. Hundert Jahre vorüber, waren die Engländer und die Amerikaner Feinde; aber heute sind sie herzlichen Freunde, Gott sei Dank! May this good-fellowship endure; may these banners here blended in amity so remain; may they never any more wave over opposing hosts, or be stained with blood which was kindred, is kindred, and always will be kindred, until a line drawn upon a map shall be able to say:

»This bars the ancestral blood from flowing
in the veins of the descendant!«

From MARK TWAIN *The Awful German Language*

Extract from the trial testimony of Charles Manson 1970

We were drawn to this speech because of the beauty of Manson's words when compared to the severity of his actions. His speech is a wonderful example of the power of rhetoric and the persuasive ability of speech. His words make it easy to lower your guard and become sympathetic to his thought process. It is worth noting that throughout his trial he was not allowed to address the jury himself out of fear of the power of his persuasive ability.

When designing and producing our piece we approached the concept on two levels. Firstly, by means of the double-sided print which can only be wholly interpreted when viewed on a lightbox. We wanted to physically separate the beauty of Manson's speech from his crimes, and it is only when the lightbox is switched on that the design becomes complete and reveals both sides of Manson's character. Typography can mimic the power of rhetoric, and the viewer needs to be cautious not to take the written word on surface value.

all our own prisons,
we are each all our
own wardens and we do our own time.
I can't judge anyone else.

in your mind...
Can't you see I'm free?

Simon Waterfall

Speech to the Institute of Directors Convention
Gerald Ratner, Royal Albert Hall 1991

Gerald Ratner, the former retail tycoon, is responsible for one of the most famous gaffes in corporate history. Once a fixture on British High Streets, Ratners was a nationwide chain of cut-price jewellers. But Mr Ratner effectively killed the company in 1991 with a speech to the Institute of Directors, when he joked that one of his firm's products was "total crap", and boasted that some of its earrings were "cheaper than a prawn sandwich from Marks and Spencer's, which would probably last longer".

The speech, instantly seized upon by the media, wiped an estimated £500m from the value of the company. Mr Ratner left the firm the following year, and his name was expunged from the company in 1994.

The photography for the poster is by Matt Mitchell.

Andrew Wilson Lambeth

ConsiderS
Jim Crace: Continent 1986

This is a text about money, about wealth. The copy I've played with from Jim Crace's first novel Continent points an oily, schoolmasterly finger at wealth's corrupting privilege, its petulant impatience, maybe even its insufficiency. Here is a sum, simple enough for thickos to get their heads round, that adds up to a flat and unmotivating promise of more of the same: comfort. Clunky schoolwork, no more sophisticated than a bike shed drug deal. And all the more need for moneymen to dress it up in priestliness and obfuscation.

I hoped to find the sly mockery of it in ironic designs: the display letters of the bastard font I drew want to be beautiful but fail ridiculously: the swashes are in the wrong places, wrongly entangled, broken-backed and fainting in coils. Busy, bad letters. But where else do we come across similarly obtuse flagrancies of penmanship? All over our money is where. On our banknotes. In those old ledgers and accounts. Inside the junk mail prize notifications. In the commercial and currency marks of the fonts on our keyboards. Stupid swash letters are the petty pomps of banking and accountancy.

I drew the font with a small repertoire of old renaissance swashes and then copied them out in neat lines onto a page of school exercise paper.

consider your inheritances : enumerate and evaluate : you are the sons
and daughters of rich men : who else but rich fathers could spare the
money for tuition fees · for examination bribes · for graduation ceremonies
calculate the value of those businesses : the import-export companies
the arms trade syndicates · the truck and bus firms · the riverside farming
enterprises · the chicken and egg franchises · the rest house chains · the
strings of market booths : include also the lands in town and country · the
houses in the new extension · the investments in foreign banks : subtract
all personal bequests and divide the remainder by the number of sons and
daughters born to your parents · and there you have it · a nice fat sum · your
inheritance : do not wish your parents dead · long life and wisdom to them
all · but be carefree · they cannot live for ever · and when they die your
comforts are assured : for you this is one world · you are internationalists
this too is your inheritance : there are no frontiers to your ambition

Winterbach Fehlschlag
Die Feuerrade
Joseph Goebbels, Berlin
10 May 1933

Matthew Di Gesu, diventar pazzo,
Ognum' gridi com' io grido,
Sempre pazzo, pazzo, pazzo.

The thousands of Girolamo Savonarola's congregation raving from Florence's Duomo exclaiming "Go crazy to Jesus" were turned against the 'degeneracy' of their time. On the Piazza della Signora, art and books were burnt, frivolity and false hair added to the Bonfire of the Vanities. Political revolution, repression, restoration of religion and morality were preached from the pulpit, and a neurotic people castigated by a powerful oration charged with unspeakable violence and destruction. Only four years later Savonarola, disregarding a papal charge of heresy, was tortured, hung and burnt on the very same spot as the original pyre that he himself had masterminded and torched. This was the middle of the 15th century.

Mark "Beauty is an attribute of the rightness and fitness in construction. Construction is the basis of all organic and organised form: the structure of a rose are no less logical than the construction of a racing car – both appeal to us for their ultimate economy and precision. Thus the striving for purity of form is the common denominator of all endeavor. In every individual activity we recognize the single way, the goal: Unity of Life!"
Berlin 1928, publisher for the Educational Alliance of German Printers.

Luke 10 May 1933, it rained in Berlin. Twenty thousand books were collected during that day by students and storm troopers on the orders of Dr Josef Goebbels. "The phoenix of a new spirit would arise from the ashes". At midnight the little doctor left a sodden and dwindling crowd, contemplating the daftness of this book-burning Nazi spectacle. It certainly signaled the beginning of the decline of a once great European cultural city. All together now (sing) "I swear by God this sacred Oath. I will render unconditional obedience to the Führer and give my life at any time for this Oath."

John "The New Typography's intolerant attitude certainly corresponds in particular to the German inclination to the absolute, its military will-to-order and its claim to sole power correspond to those fearful components of German-ness which unleashed Hitler's rule and the Second World War."

Jan Tschichold, Switzerland 1946.

For PUBLIC ADDRESS SYSTEM exhibition at the Henry Peacock Gallery London
Poster Speeches by 40 typographers 9.1.04 - 14.2.04

JOSEPH GOEBBELS
The Ministry of Public Enlightenment and Propaganda. Mob Orator and Nazi Servant

DIE FEURREDE

**May 10 1933. Deutsche Stattsoper, Berlin –
the regime consigned decadent works to the flames**

Deutsche Studenten: Wir haben unsere Handeln gegen den undeutschen Geist gerichtet; übergebt alles undeutschen dem Feuer, gegen Klassenkampf und Materialismus, für Volksgemeinschaft und idealistische Lebenshaltung. Ich übergebe dem Feuer die Schriften von **Karl Marx und Kautsky**.

Gegen Dekadenz und moralischen Verfall! Für Zucht und Sitte in Familie und Staat! Ich übergebe dem Feuer die Schriften von **Heinrich Mann, Glaeser, Erich Kästner**.

Gegen Gesinnungslumperei und politischen Verrat, für Hingabe an Volk und Staat! Ich übergebe dem Feuer die Schriften des **Friedrich Wilhelm Förster**.

Gegen seelenzerfasernde Überschätzung des Trieblebens, für den Adel der menschlichen Seele! Ich übergebe dem Feuer die Schriften des **Sigmund Freud.**

Gegen Verfälschung unserer Geschichte und Herabwürdigung ihrer großen Gestalten, für Ehrfurcht vor unserer Vergangenheit! Ich übergebe dem Feuer die Schriften des **Emil Ludwig Kohn und Werner Hegemann.**

Gegen volksfremden Journalismus demokratisch-jüdischer Prägung, für verantwortungsbewusste Mitarbeit am Werk des nationalen Aufbaus! Ich übergebe dem Feuer die Schriften des **Theodor Wolff und Bernhard.**

Gegen literarischen Verrat am Soldaten des Weltkrieges, für Erziehung des Volkes im Geist der Wahrhaftigkeit! Ich übergebe dem Feuer die Schriften des **Remarque.**

Gegen dünkelhafte Verhunzung der deutschen Sprache, für Pflege des kostbarsten Gutes unseres Volkes! Ich übergebe dem Feuer die Schriften des **Alfred Kerr.**

Gegen Frechheit und Anmaßung, für Achtung und Ehrfurcht vor dem unsterblichen deutschen Volksgeist. Verschlinge, Feuer, auch Schriften der **Tucholsky, Ossietzky!**

Against class conflict, I hand over the writings of Karl Marx and Kautsky to the fire. For political betrayal, I hand over the writings of Friedrich Wilhelm Förster to the fire. For the aristocracy of the human soul, I hand over the writings of Freud to the fire. For respect for our past, I hand over the writings of Kohn and Hegemann to the fire. Against Jewish-democratic-influenced journalism, I hand over the writings of Wolff and Bernhard to the fire. For literary betrayal of our soldiers I hand over the writings of Remarque to the fire. **Against the debasement of the German language** I hand over the writings of Kerr to the fire. Devour fire, the work of Tucholsky & Ossietzky!

GOEBBELS OR GOBBELS

(Paul) Joseph [Goebels] 1897-1945 politician
b. Rheydt Germany
Deformed foot absolved him from military service
Anti-semite
As youth attended many universities
Powerful exponent of the radical aspects of Nazi philosophy. When Hitler was running the war Goebbels was running the country.

The unacceptable to the new order
Albert Einstein
Sigmund Freud
Erich Maria Remarque
Carl von Ossietzky
Kurt Tucholsky
Hugo von Hofmannsthal
Erich Kästner
Carl Zuckmayer
Karl Marx etc
Bertolt Brecht wrote a poem Die Bücherverbrennung
(The Book Burning)
demanding that the
regime burn him,
since it had
not burnt
his writings and
so he was therefore
denied this incendiary
public recognition.

**'Where books
are burnt in the end people are also burnt'
Heinrich Heine**

Winterbach-Fehlschlag

The New Typography (Berlin 1928) A Modern Handbook: was the vision of a man from Leipzig who was convinced that his beliefs were the only truth, and that the sooner they were recognized by everyone the better and purer life would be. It was also necessary to sweep away the 'rubbish' of the past.

info@henrypeacock.com. Telephone 020 7323 4033   **12.**00
TO
Gallery opening Wednesday to Saturday only   **6.**00
PM   ➡

Organiser Angharad Lewis

CONSIDERH
ENUMERATEE
EVALUATEF
CALCULATE
THEVALUEH
NINCLUDEH
SUBTRACTH
HDIVIDEH
REMAINDER
OTHERETHN
HAVEITHIN
HERITANCE
WORLDHNO
FRONTIERS

TOGETHER WE ARE ROBOTS

U.S.U.K The United States of the United Kingdom

You can dictate
just about anywh
you can type.

"the announce-ments of music halls, movies, the promotion of cigarettes the fervor of business advertising – their nightly blaze above Potsdamer Platz – drown, suffocate, and obliterate any of the political battle cries in an inferno of light and noise and colour."

Joseph Roth

Contributors' Speeches

The following speeches have been chosen by the organisers of Public Address System and by the contributors to this book. Reproducing these speeches here constitutes an exercise. It emulates the decision-making processes that the designers who partook in the exhibition underwent in the creation of their posters, but from a non-design perspective. What follows is a study of how words alone on a page conventionally represent speech. The choices of the contributors have come at the end of several individuals' experiences of being involved in the Public Address System project and are thus informed by a prolonged spell of thinking about and engaging with the idea of speech, its functions, and the modes of representation used to communicate speech.

Henry V addressing the troops at the Battle of Agincourt

William Shakespeare: Henry V 1599

Once more unto the breach, dear friends, once more;
Or close the wall up with our English dead.
In peace there's nothing so becomes a man
As modest stillness and humility:
But when the blast of war blows in our ears,
Then imitate the action of the tiger;
Stiffen the sinews, summon up the blood,
Disguise fair nature with hard-favour'd rage;
Then lend the eye a terrible aspect;
Let pry through the portage of the head
Like the brass cannon; let the brow o'erwhelm it
As fearfully as doth a galled rock
O'erhang and jutty his confounded base,
Swill'd with the wild and wasteful ocean.
Now set the teeth and stretch the nostril wide,
Hold hard the breath and bend up every spirit
To his full height. On, on, you noblest English.
Whose blood is fet from fathers of war-proof!
Fathers that, like so many Alexanders,
Have in these parts from morn till even fought
And sheathed their swords for lack of argument:
Dishonour not your mothers; now attest
That those whom you call'd fathers did beget you.
Be copy now to men of grosser blood,
And teach them how to war. And you, good yeoman,
Whose limbs were made in England, show us here
The mettle of your pasture; let us swear
That you are worth your breeding; which I doubt not;

For there is none of you so mean and base,
That hath not noble lustre in your eyes.
I see you stand like greyhounds in the slips,
Straining upon the start. The game's afoot:
Follow your spirit, and upon this charge
Cry 'God for Harry, England, and Saint George!'

Henry V's speech to his troops before the Battle of Agincourt, courtesy of Shakespeare, is perhaps not the most obvious choice for a Parliamentarian who voted against the war in Iraq. Nevertheless, this is truly the mother of all battle speeches and apart from humour it has it all – passion, honesty, a theme, a beginning, a middle and an end. No doubt at all, that by the end of it, those lads knew why they were there in that field in France.

—John Grogan MP

Neil Kinnock, Bridgend
7 June 1983

If Margaret Thatcher is re-elected as Prime Minister,
I warn you.

I warn you that you will have pain:
When healing and relief depend upon payment.
I warn you that you will have ignorance:
When talents are untended and wits are wasted, when
learning is a privilege and not a right.

I warn you that you will have poverty:
When pensions slip and benefits are whittled away by a
Government that won't pay in an economy that can't pay.
I warn you that you will be cold:
When fuel charges are used as a tax system that the rich
don't notice and the poor can't afford.

I warn you that you must not expect work:
When many cannot spend, more will not be able to earn.
When they don't earn, they don't spend.
When they don't spend, work dies.
I warn you not to go into the streets alone after dark
or into the streets in large crowds of protest in the light.

I warn you that you will be quiet:
When the curfew of fear and the gibbet of unemployment
make you obedient.
I warn you that you will have a defense of a sort:
With a risk and at a price that passes all understanding.

I warn you that you will be home-bound:
When fares and transport bills kill leisure and lock you up.
I warn you that you will borrow less:
When credit, loans, mortgages and easy payments are
refused to people on your melting income.

If Margaret Thatcher wins, she will be more a Leader than a Prime Minister. That power produces arrogance and when it is toughened by Tebbitry and flattered and fawned upon by spineless sycophants, the boot-licking tabloid Knights of Fleet Street and placemen in the Quangos, the arrogance corrupts absolutely.

If Margaret Thatcher wins:
I warn you not to be ordinary.
I warn you not to be young.
I warn you not to fall ill.
I warn you not to get old.

For me, this is Kinnock at his most powerful: his urgency elevates his oratory to the brink of poetry and inflames his words to such a degree that they brand themselves on to the consciousness of his audience. Whether or not you agree with him, the authenticity of the man is unmistakable: a genuine conviction politician.

—Ayesha Mohideen

Declaration of the Rights of Women

Olympe de Gouge 1791

Women, wake up; the tocsin of reason is being heard throughout the whole universe; discover your rights. The powerful empire of nature is no longer surrounded by prejudice, fanaticism, superstition, and lies. The flame of truth has dispersed all the clouds of folly and usurpation. Enslaved man has multiplied his strength and needs recourse to yours to break his chains. Having become free, he has become unjust to his companion. Oh, women, women! When will you cease to be blind? What advantage have you received from the Revolution? A more pronounced scorn, a more marked disdain. In the centuries of corruption you ruled only over the weakness of men. The reclamation of your patrimony, based on the wise decrees of nature – what have you to dread from such a fine undertaking? The bon mot of the legislator of the marriage of Cana? Do you fear that our French legislators, correctors of that morality, long ensnared by political practices now out of date, will only say to you: women, what is there in common between you and us? Everything, you will have to answer. If they persist in their weakness in putting this non sequitur in contradiction to their principles, courageously oppose the force of reason to the empty pretensions of superiority; unite yourselves beneath the standards of philosophy; deploy all the energy of your character, and you will soon see these haughty men, not grovelling at your feet as servile adorers, but proud to share with you the treasures of the Supreme Being. Regardless of what barriers confront you, it is in your power to free yourselves; you have only to want to.

The process of selecting a speech that holds some kind of importance to you is more challenging than it looks, and I was disturbed to see that out of all those selected, not one had been by a woman. This can perhaps in part be attributed to the way in which history has been documented, so my choice therefore is an attempt to readdress the balance.

I wanted to find a speech whose words had empowered people into action, and came across the 18th-century revolutionary, Olympe de Gouge, a butcher's daughter whose words led her to her own execution by the guillotine in 1793.

Her 'Declaration of the Rights of Women' was a direct challenge to the inferiority presumed of women by the 'Declaration of the Rights of Man', and has a tone that is brash yet eloquent, dated yet surprisingly modern, and a power that encapsulates the injustice of the situation.

—Harriet Warden

The Aim of Team Ten
Peter and Alison Smithson 1954

Team Ten is a group of architects who have sought each other out because each has found the help of others necessary to the development of their individual work. But it is more than that. They came together in the first place, certainly because of mutual realization of the inadequacies of the processes of architectural thought, which they had inherited from the modern movement as a whole, but more important, each sensed that the other had already found some way to new beginning. This new beginning and the long build-up that followed, has been concerned with inducing, as it were, into the blood stream of the architect an understanding and feeling for the patterns, the aspirations, the artifacts, the tools, the modes of transportation and communications of present-day society, so that he can, as a natural thing, build towards society's realization of itself.

In this sense Team Ten is utopian, but utopian about the present. Thus their aim is not to theorize but to build, for only through construction can a utopia of the present be realised. For them 'to build' has a special meaning in that the architect's responsibility, towards the individual or groups he builds for and towards the cohesion and convenience of the collective structure to which they belong, is taken as being an absolute responsibility. No abstract master plan stands between him and what he has to do, only the 'human facts' and the logistics of the situation. To accept such responsibility, where none is trying to direct others to perform acts which his control techniques cannot encompass, requires the invention of working-together-techniques where each pays attention to the other and to the whole in so far as he is able.

Team Ten is of the opinion that only in such a way may meaningful groupings of buildings come into being, where each building is a live thing and a natural extension of the others; together they will make places where a man can realise what he wishes to be.

Team Ten would like to develop their thought processes and language of building to a point where a collective demonstration could be made at a scale, which would be really effective in terms of the modes of life and the structure of a community.

Team Ten were formed in 1953 at CIAM (Congres International d'Architecture Moderne) Ten by Alison and Peter Smithson, architects of the house of the future 1954, Hunstanton Secondary Modern school in 1953, brutalist architects.

Why I chose this speech

1. A continuation of the modernist project – for architecture read any discipline – a reinvigoration of the central tenets, a natural response to the birth of the consumer culture of the 50s/60s within the modernist project.

2. A genuine concern for the way people lead their lives, not some patrician snobbish attitude to the users of this architecture.

3. A call for a quiet, understated, theoretically rigorous and well-built architecture, no master plans but no horrible relativist post-modern pastiches of historicist styles, no unambitious piecemeal reforms.

4. To talk about design as a 'live' thing, to understand the great architecture of the past and to show it true respect by attempting to learn the lessons and not simply to pastiche or copy it.

5. To talk about the collective and community without some kind of limp reactionary or leftist nostalgia for halycon days.

—Aidan Winterburn

The Tragedy of Human Effort

CH Douglas, Central Hall, Liverpool
30 October 1936

I suppose that there can be few amongst those of us who think about the world in which we live, and, perhaps, fewer amongst the more obvious victims of it, who would not agree that its condition is serious and shows every sign of becoming worse. Many must have asked themselves why the ability of scientists, organisers and educationists, brilliant and laudable in essence, seem to lead us only from one catastrophe to another, until it would appear knowledge, invention, and progress, so far from being our salvation, have doomed the world to almost inevitable destruction.

How is it that in 1495 the labourer was able to maintain himself in a standard of living considerably higher, relatively to his generation, than that of the present time, with only fifty days' labour a year, whereas now millions are working in an age of marvellous machinery the whole year round, in an effort to maintain themselves and their families just above the line of destitution?

Why is it that 150 years ago the percentage of the population which could be economically classed as middle and upper classes was two or three times that which it is at the present time? Why is it that while production per man-hour has risen forty or fifty times at least in the past hundred years, the wages of the fully employed have risen only about four times, and the average wage of the employable is considerably less than four times that of a hundred years ago, measured in real commodities? How is it that the nations are given over to the dictatorship of men of gangster mentality, whose proper place is in a Borstal institution?

I have very little doubt that there are numbers of people in this room who could at once give a correct general answer to the preceding questions, and that it would take the form of an indictment of the financial system: and I should, of course, agree with this answer up to a certain point. They might add that no inventor is left in control of his invention, and that the financial octopus seizes everything with is slimy tentacles and turn it to its own use.

We are the poorer today: is this metaphor? In Douglas's mind it is not metaphor. The quality of our lives, and our freedom: that is our wealth. Your riches should be reckoned by your store of time and energy, and will be diminished by any encroachment upon these. Douglas knew it, I know it and because of this opportunity to choose a speech I thought you'd better know it.

—Thom Winterburn

Editors:
Paul Finn is a freelance designer.
Angharad Lewis is deputy editor of Grafik magazine and a director of Grafik Ltd.
Harriet Warden is a freelance arts administrator currently working with Tate.
Thom Winterburn is founder of the Henry Peacock Gallery, The Henry Peacock Press and Jeffrey Charles Henry Peacock.

Published in Australia in 2006 by
The Images Publishing Group Pty Ltd
ABN 89 059 734 431
6 Bastow Place, Mulgrave, Victoria 3170, Australia
Tel: +61 3 9561 5544 Fax: +61 3 9561 4860
books@images.com.au
www.imagespublishing.com

Copyright © The Images Publishing Group Pty Ltd 2006
The Images Publishing Group Reference Number: 693

National Library of Australia Cataloguing-in-Publication entry:

Public Address System: poster speeches by typographers.

ISBN 1 86470 188 9.
ISBN 978 1 86470 188 3.

1. Posters – 21st century. 2. Posters, English.
3. Typographers – Great Britain. I. Finn, Paul.
II. Public Address System.

741.674
Typography and graphic design by Paulus M Dreibholz, London/Vienna

Printed by Paramount Printing Company Limited Hong Kong

IMAGES has included on its website a page for special notices in relation to this and its other publications. Please visit: www.imagespublishing.com